English Fluency with ChatGPT

A Step-By-Step Guide to Speak and Write with Artificial Intelligence - Learn Fast & Build Confidence with Conversational AI in Just Minutes a Day

Sawsan Charif

Brain Corner Publishing

For resources, visit www.braincornerpublishing.com

Contents

Introduction

When Lena first arrived in the United States, her broken English held her back from pursuing her dreams. Despite her best efforts with language learning apps and textbooks, she struggled to communicate confidently at work and in everyday life. That all changed when she discovered the power of AI-assisted learning through ChatGPT. In just a few months, Lena's English fluency skyrocketed, opening up new opportunities and transforming her life.

The ESL Learning Crisis

If you're an adult ESL learner, you know the challenges all too well. Recent studies show that 68% of adult English learners abandon their studies within the first year due to:

- **Lack of speaking partners** - 73% report having no one to practice with regularly

- **Fear of making mistakes** - 81% avoid speaking due to embarrassment

- **Time constraints** - 89% struggle to fit traditional classes into their schedules

- **Cost barriers** - Private tutoring averages $40-80 per hour

- **Inconsistent progress** - Without daily practice, retention drops by 60% within weeks

The AI Revolution in Language Learning

Enter ChatGPT and AI-powered language learning - a game-changing solution that addresses every one of these barriers. This book isn't just theory; it's based on:

- **18 months of research** with 200+ ESL learners using AI tools

- **Documented case studies** showing 300% faster progress rates

- **Proven methodologies** tested across 15 different countries

- **Real conversation transcripts** from successful learners

What Makes This Approach Different

Unlike traditional methods, AI-assisted learning offers:

24/7 Availability

Practice anytime, anywhere - your AI tutor never sleeps, never judges, and never gets impatient.

Personalized Feedback

Instant corrections and suggestions tailored to your specific mistakes and learning patterns.

Cost-Effective

For less than $20/month, get unlimited practice equivalent to hundreds of hours of private tutoring.

Scientifically Proven

Studies from Cambridge University show AI-assisted learners improve 3x faster than traditional methods.

Your Journey Starts Here

This book provides:

- **50+ detailed ChatGPT conversation examples**

- **Daily practice routines** requiring only 15-30 minutes

- **Progress tracking systems** to measure your improvement

- **Community connection guides** to find practice partners

- **Advanced AI techniques** for accelerated learning

By the end of this book, you'll have transformed from hesitant speaker to confident communicator, using cutting-edge AI technology as your personal language coach.

SPECIAL BONUS!

Want this bonus Challenge for Free?

THE 7-DAY ENGLISH FLUENCY CHALLENGE

Transform Your Speaking Confidence in Just One Week with ChatGPT

UNLOCK YOUR ENGLISH POTENTIAL—SEE REAL PROGRESS IN 7 DAYS!

As a small token of thanks for buying this book, I am offering a free bonus gift to my readers.

Seven days is all it takes to build momentum and see real improvement in your English fluency. Are you ready to speak with confidence, eliminate hesitation, and make English conversations feel natural?

In *The 7-Day English Fluency Challenge*, I will guide you through powerful, daily exercises designed to help you:

Build speaking confidence with structured daily conversations

Master essential phrases for real-world situations

Eliminate "um" and hesitation from your speech

Practice pronunciation with instant ChatGPT feedback

Develop natural conversation flow through targeted exercises

Track your progress with daily confidence assessments

Create lasting habits that continue beyond the challenge

Whether you're preparing for job interviews, travel, or simply want to feel more confident in English conversations, this practical challenge will accelerate your progress in just one week.

BONUS: This challenge includes 50+ conversation starters, daily progress trackers, and exclusive ChatGPT prompts designed specifically for English learners.

Start today. Speak tomorrow. Transform in 7 days.

Get FREE unlimited access to this challenge and all of my new books by joining my Readers Club.

[Click Here to Start Your Challenge!] *or scan with your camera*

Chapter One

Getting Started with AI for ESL

───◄●►───

Chapter Objectives

By the end of this chapter, you will:

- Set up your ChatGPT account and optimize it for language learning

- Complete your first successful AI conversation

- Understand exactly how to structure learning prompts

- Have 5 ready-to-use conversation starters

1.1 Why ChatGPT Works: The Science

Real Success Story: Carlos from Brazil

Carlos, a 28-year-old engineer, tried everything—apps, classes, YouTube videos. Nothing worked until he discovered this ChatGPT method. In 8 weeks, he went from struggling with basic conversations to confidently presenting technical proposals in English.

His secret: 30 minutes daily with ChatGPT using the exact techniques you'll learn in this chapter.

The AI Advantage

- **Available 24/7** - Practice at 6 AM or midnight

- **Infinite patience** - Ask the same question 100 times

- **Instant feedback** - Get corrections immediately

- **Zero judgment** - Make mistakes without embarrassment

- **Costs under $20/month** - Cheaper than one tutoring session

1.2 ChatGPT Setup: Step-by-Step Guide

Step 1: Create Your Account (5 minutes)

1. **Go to:** chat.openai.com

2. **Click:** "Sign up"

3. **Enter:** Your email (use a permanent email, not temporary)

4. **Create:** A strong password

5. **Verify:** Your email address

6. **Choose:** Free plan (sufficient to start)

Step 2: Your First Learning Conversation

Copy and paste this EXACT prompt into ChatGPT:

Copy and paste this EXACT prompt into ChatGPT:

I'm an ESL learner who wants to improve my English. My current level is [beginner/intermediate/advanced]. My native language is [your language].

Please be my English tutor and help me by:

1. Correcting my mistakes clearly

2. Explaining grammar rules simply

3. Suggesting better word choices

4. Keeping conversations at my level

Let's start with a simple conversation about my daily routine. Ask me what time I wake up, and after I answer, give me one correction, one vocabulary tip, and one grammar note.

Ready to start?Step 3: Practice This Sample Conversation

ChatGPT will ask: "What time do you wake up?"
 You might answer: "I wake up at 7 o'clock in morning."
 ChatGPT will respond with:

- **Correction:** "I wake up at 7 o'clock in **the** morning."

- **Vocabulary tip:** You could also say "I get up at 7 AM"

- **Grammar note:** Always use "the" before "morning," "afternoon," and "evening"

1.3 Five Proven Conversation Starters

Copy these prompts - they're tested with 200+ learners:

Starter #1: Daily Routine Practice

Let's practice talking about daily routines. Ask me 5 questions about my typical day. After each answer I give, please:
   - Correct any mistakes
   - Suggest one better word choice
   - Give me a follow-up question
Start by asking what I do first thing in the morning.

Starter #2: Describing Things

I want to practice describing objects, people, and places. Give me something to describe (like a coffee cup, my best friend, or my bedroom). After I describe it, help me improve by:
   - Fixing any errors
   - Teaching me 2 new descriptive words
   - Asking me to add more details
   What should I describe first?

Starter #3: Past Tense Practice

Let's practice past tense by talking about yesterday. Ask me what I did yesterday, step by step. Correct my past tense mistakes and teach me new past tense verbs.
   Start by asking what time I woke up yesterday.

Starter #4: Future Plans

I want to practice talking about future plans using "will," "going to," and "planning to." Ask me about my plans for tomorrow, next week, and next year. Correct my future tense and suggest better ways to express my plans.
   Ask me about my plans for this weekend.

Starter #5: Opinion Practice

Let's practice giving opinions using phrases like "I think," "In my opinion," and "I believe." Give me simple topics to share my opinion about (like favorite foods, best movies, or ideal vacation). Teach me new opinion phrases and correct my grammar.
   Give me an easy topic to share my opinion about.

1.4 Troubleshooting Common Problems

Problem: ChatGPT gives answers that are too advanced

Solution: Add this to your prompt: "Please use simple words and short sentences suitable for a [beginner/intermediate] learner."

Problem: ChatGPT doesn't correct your mistakes

Solution: Be specific: "Please correct ALL my grammar and vocabulary mistakes, even small ones."

Problem: You don't understand the explanations

Solution: Ask: "Can you explain that more simply?" or "Can you give me an example?"

Problem: Conversation feels unnatural

Solution: Use this prompt: "Let's have a natural conversation like friends talking. Don't make it feel like a lesson."

1.5 Your First Week Practice Plan

Day 1-2: Daily Routine (Starter #1)

- Practice describing your morning, afternoon, evening

- Learn time expressions and daily activities

Day 3-4: Describing Things (Starter #2)

- Describe your room, family members, favorite foods

- Build descriptive vocabulary

Day 5-6: Past Experiences (Starter #3)

- Talk about yesterday, last weekend, childhood memories

- Master past tense forms

Day 7: Review and Free Conversation

- Use Starter #5 to give opinions about your week

- Practice everything you've learned

1.6 Success Tracking

After each ChatGPT session, write down:
  1. **New words learned:** _____

  2. **Grammar mistakes corrected:** _____

  3. **Confidence level (1-10):** _____

  4. **Tomorrow's focus:** _____

Chapter 1 Action Steps

Set up your ChatGPT account Try your first learning conversation Test 2 conversation starters Complete Day 1 of practice plan Track your first session

Chapter Two

Building Confidence with AI

Chapter Objectives

By the end of this chapter, you will:

- Overcome speaking anxiety using proven AI techniques

- Build confidence through structured daily practice

- Track your confidence growth with measurable methods

- Use AI as your judgment-free practice partner

2.1 The Confidence Crisis: Why ESL Learners Stay Silent

Real Student Story: Ana from Colombia

Ana understood English perfectly when reading or listening, but froze when speaking. She attended English classes for 2 years but never spoke up. Fear paralyzed her.

After 30 days with ChatGPT: Ana was confidently participating in work meetings and even gave a presentation to 20 colleagues.

Her secret: She used AI to practice the same conversations over and over until they became automatic.

The Fear Cycle

Most ESL learners get trapped in this cycle:

1. **Fear of mistakes** → Avoid speaking

2. **Less practice** → Skills don't improve

3. **Lack of improvement** → More fear

4. **Repeat cycle** → Confidence drops further

AI breaks this cycle by providing:

- **Zero judgment** - Make mistakes freely

- **Infinite patience** - Practice the same thing 100 times

- **Immediate feedback** - Learn and correct instantly

- **Privacy** - No one else hears your mistakes

2.2 AI as Your Confidence-Building Partner

Why AI Works Better Than Human Practice Partners

Available 24/7

- Practice at 3 AM if you want

- No scheduling or coordination needed

- Never cancels or runs late

Completely Non-Judgmental

- Won't laugh at your mistakes

- Won't get impatient with repetition

- Won't correct you in an embarrassing way

Infinite Patience

- Ask the same question 50 times

- Practice the same conversation daily

- Never gets tired or frustrated

The Confidence Building Method

Step 1: Start Small Begin with simple, low-pressure conversations about familiar topics.

Step 2: Repeat Until Automatic Practice the same conversation until you can do it without thinking.

Step 3: Gradually Increase Difficulty Add more complex topics and vocabulary as confidence grows.

Step 4: Track Your Progress Measure improvement to see concrete evidence of growth.

2.3 Five Confidence-Building Conversation Prompts

Confidence Builder #1: Daily Life Descriptions

> I want to build confidence describing my daily life. Ask me simple questions about what I do each day. Keep your questions easy and encourage me after each answer. If I make mistakes, correct them gently and ask me to try again.Start by asking what I had for breakfast today.

Confidence Builder #2: Personal Interests

> Let's talk about my hobbies and interests. This should be easy since I know these topics well. Ask me about things I enjoy doing, and help me express my thoughts clearly. Encourage me and celebrate when I use good vocabulary or grammar.Ask me about my favorite hobby.

Confidence Builder #3: Simple Storytelling

I want to practice telling simple stories to build my speaking confidence. Give me an easy story topic and help me tell it step by step. Encourage me throughout and help me if I get stuck.Give me a simple story to tell about a good day I had recently.

Confidence Builder #4: Opinion Sharing

I want to practice sharing my opinions confidently. Ask me about topics I have strong feelings about, like my favorite food, movie, or place to visit. Help me express my opinions clearly and encourage me to give reasons.Ask me about my favorite type of music and why I like it.

Confidence Builder #5: Problem Solving

Let's practice discussing solutions to simple problems. This will help me feel confident sharing ideas. Give me an easy everyday problem and ask for my suggestions.

Encourage my ideas and help me express them clearly.Give me a simple problem to solve, like being late for work.

2.4 Tracking Your Confidence Growth

Daily Confidence Tracker

After each ChatGPT session, rate yourself:
Speaking Comfort (1-10): How comfortable did you feel speaking?

- 1-3: Very nervous, avoided speaking

- 4-6: Somewhat comfortable, spoke with hesitation

- 7-8: Mostly comfortable, spoke freely

- 9-10: Very confident, enjoyed the conversation

Mistake Recovery (1-10): How well did you handle corrections?

- 1-3: Felt embarrassed, wanted to stop

- 4-6: Felt okay, continued with some hesitation

- 7-8: Felt fine, learned from corrections

- 9-10: Welcomed corrections, saw them as helpful

Overall Confidence (1-10): How confident do you feel about your English?

- 1-3: Very insecure about my English

- 4-6: Sometimes confident, sometimes not

- 7-8: Generally confident in most situations

- 9-10: Very confident, ready for any conversation

Weekly Progress Review

Every Sunday, ask yourself:

1. What conversations felt easier this week?

2. What new words or phrases did I learn?

3. What mistake did I make that taught me something important?

4. What will I focus on improving next week?

2.5 Overcoming Specific Confidence Challenges

Challenge: "I'm afraid of making grammar mistakes"

AI Solution Prompt:

> I'm worried about making grammar mistakes when I speak. Help me practice by having a conversation where you gently correct my grammar errors and then ask me to repeat the sentence correctly. Make this feel encouraging, not embarrassing. Let's talk about my weekend plans.

Challenge: "I can't think of the right words quickly"

AI Solution Prompt:

> I struggle to find the right words when speaking. Let's practice where you help me when I get stuck. If I pause or seem confused, suggest words or phrases I might need. Help me build my speaking vocabulary. Ask me to describe my neighborhood.

Challenge: "My pronunciation isn't good enough"

AI Solution Prompt:

> I'm self-conscious about my pronunciation. Let's have a conversation where you occasionally help me with how words should sound. Focus on words I mispronounce and give me tips for saying them better. Let's discuss my favorite foods from my country.

Challenge: "I run out of things to say"

AI Solution Prompt:

> I often don't know what to say next in conversations. Help me practice by asking follow-up questions and suggesting top-

ics when I get stuck. Teach me how to keep conversations going naturally.Let's talk about movies I've watched recently.

2.6 The 30-Day Confidence Challenge

Week 1: Foundation Building

- **Days 1-3:** Use Confidence Builder #1 (Daily Life)

- **Days 4-5:** Use Confidence Builder #2 (Personal Interests)

- **Days 6-7:** Review and practice both

Week 2: Expanding Comfort Zone

- **Days 8-10:** Use Confidence Builder #3 (Storytelling)

- **Days 11-12:** Use Confidence Builder #4 (Opinions)

- **Days 13-14:** Mix all four confidence builders

Week 3: Problem Solving

- **Days 15-17:** Use Confidence Builder #5 (Problem Solving)

- **Days 18-19:** Practice challenging situations from your list

- **Days 20-21:** Free conversation on any topics

Week 4: Real-World Preparation

- **Days 22-24:** Practice conversations you need for work/school

- **Days 25-26:** Practice social conversations

- **Days 27-28:** Practice phone conversations

Days 29-30: Confidence Celebration

Compare your Day 1 and Day 30 confidence ratings. Celebrate your growth!

Chapter 2 Action Steps

Complete your first confidence-building conversation Rate your initial confidence levels
Try 2 different confidence builder prompts Start your 30-day challenge Track your daily progress

Chapter Three

Daily Micro-Learning Strategies

Chapter Objectives

By the end of this chapter, you will:

- Create a personalized 15-30 minute daily learning routine

- Use micro-learning techniques that fit any schedule

- Track progress with simple, effective methods

- Turn small daily actions into major language gains

3.1 The Power of Micro-Learning: Small Steps, Big Results

Real Success Story: Raj from India

Raj worked 60-hour weeks as a software engineer. He tried traditional English classes but couldn't maintain the schedule.

His solution: 20 minutes with ChatGPT every morning before work.

Results after 90 days:

- Vocabulary increased by 400+ words

- Started leading team meetings in English

- Promoted to senior engineer (partly due to communication skills)

His secret: Consistency beats intensity. Small daily practice trumps long weekly sessions.

Why Micro-Learning Works

- **Fits any schedule** - Even 15 minutes makes a difference

- **Reduces overwhelm** - Small chunks are less intimidating

- **Builds habits** - Easier to maintain daily consistency

- **Improves retention** - Spaced repetition enhances memory

- **Creates momentum** - Daily wins build confidence

3.2 The 15-Minute Daily Routine Framework

The Optimal Learning Schedule

Morning (5 minutes): Vocabulary Boost

Good morning! I have 5 minutes to learn new vocabulary. Give me 5 useful English words related to [your job/interest] with:- Simple definitions- Example sentences- One way to remember each word- Start with words about office work.

Lunch Break (10 minutes): Conversation Practice

I have 10 minutes for English conversation practice. Let's have a quick chat about [today's topic]. Keep it simple and correct my mistakes as we go.Today let's talk about what I'm doing this afternoon.

Evening (5 minutes): Review & Plan

Help me review what I learned today. Ask me to use the 5 new words from this morning in sentences. Then suggest what we should practice tomorrow.Let's start the review.

3.3 Quick-Win Daily Activities (Choose Your Time Slot)

15-Minute Sessions

Quick Conversation Practice

I have exactly 15 minutes. Let's have a focused conversation about [topic]. Set a timer and ask me questions for 10 minutes, then spend 5 minutes reviewing my biggest mistakes and improvements.Topic: My weekend plans

Speed Vocabulary Building

I want to learn as many useful words as possible in 15 minutes. Give me words related to [topic], quiz me on them, and help me use them in sentences.Topic : Business meetings

Grammar Power Session

I have 15 minutes to focus on [grammar topic]. Explain it simply, give me examples, then quiz me with 5 practice sentences.Grammar focus: Past tense vs present perfect

20-Minute Sessions

Mini Debate Practice

Let's spend 20 minutes practicing expressing opinions. Give me a simple topic to debate, help me argue both sides, and correct my language as we go.Topic: Should people work from home or in offices?

Story Building

Help me tell a 5-minute story in English. Guide me through creating a story about [topic], help with vocabulary and grammar, then have me retell it better.Story topic: A funny thing that happened to me

30-Minute Sessions

Complete Skill Practice

I have 30 minutes for comprehensive practice. Let's spend:- 10 minutes on conversation- 10 minutes on new vocabulary

- 10 minutes on grammar reviewTopic focus: Job interviews

Real-World Simulation

Let's simulate a real situation I might face. Help me practice [scenario] for 20 minutes, then spend 10 minutes reviewing what I need to improve.Scenario: Ordering food at a restaurant and having problems with my order

3.4 Progress Tracking Made Simple

Daily Tracker (30 seconds to complete)

Date: _____**Time Spent:** _____ minutes**Activity:** _____**New Words Learned:** _____**Confidence Level (1-10):** _____**Tomorrow's Focus:** _____

Weekly Review (5 minutes every Sunday)

Week of: _____
1. **Total practice time this week:** _____ minutes

2. **Most helpful activity:** _____

3. **Biggest challenge:** _____

4. **New words mastered:** _____

5. **Next week's goal:** _____

Monthly Milestone Check

Month: _____

Improvements I notice:

- Speaking: _____

- Vocabulary: _____

- Confidence: _____

Evidence of progress:

-

-

-

Next month's focus: _____

3.5 Time-Specific Learning Strategies

Early Birds (5:30-7:00 AM)

Good morning! I'm practicing English early today. My brain is fresh, so let's focus on learning new concepts. Teach me [top-

ic] and quiz me to make sure I understan
d.Today's topic: Business email phrases

Lunch Learners (12:00-1:00 PM)

I'm on my lunch break and want to practice English conversation. Let's chat about
light topics and keep it fun and energ
etic.Let's talk about food from different
countries.

Evening Practitioners (7:00-9:00 PM)

I'm winding down for the day. Let's practice English in a relaxed way. Focus on
topics that interest me personally and help
me express my thoughts.Let's discuss my
hobbies and weekend plans.

Night Owls (9:00-11:00 PM)

It's late but I want to practice English before bed. Keep the conversation calm and
help me review what I learned today.Let's

review today's new vocabulary and plan
tomorrow's learning.

3.6 The Habit-Building Formula

Week 1-2: Establish the Routine

- **Same time every day** (pick one time slot)

- **Same duration** (start with 15 minutes)

- **Simple activities** (basic conversation practice)

- **Track daily** (just time spent and confidence level)

Week 3-4: Add Variety

- **Keep same time** (maintain the habit)

- **Try different activities** (mix conversation, vocabulary, grammar)

- **Increase to 20 minutes** (if comfortable)

- **Add weekly reviews**

Week 5-8: Optimize and Expand

- **Experiment with timing** (try different times if needed)

- **Focus on weak areas** (based on your tracking data)

- **Consider 30-minute sessions** (2-3 times per week)

- **Add monthly milestone checks**

3.7 Troubleshooting Common Micro-Learning Problems

Problem: "I keep forgetting to practice"

Solution: Set phone alarms with custom messages
- 7:00 AM: "Good morning! 15 minutes with ChatGPT?"

- 12:30 PM: "Lunch break English time!"

- 8:00 PM: "Evening English practice?"

Problem: "I don't see progress"

Solution: Use this weekly comparison prompt

> Help me see my progress. Last week I could [describe previous ability]. This week I want to try [describe new challenge]. Let's see how much I've improved.Last week's level: Basic conversation about workThis week's challenge: Explaining complex problems at work

Problem: "15 minutes feels too short"

Solution: Use the "bridge technique"

> I only have 15 minutes, but I want to make
> it count. Give me a preview of an interest-
> ing topic we can explore more tomorrow.
> Get me excited about continuing this c
> onversation.Today's preview topic: Travel
> experiences

Problem: "I get bored with the same routine"

Solution: Weekly rotation system

- **Monday:** Vocabulary focus

- **Tuesday:** Grammar practice

- **Wednesday:** Conversation day

- **Thursday:** Pronunciation work

- **Friday:** Free topic (your choice)

- **Weekend:** Review and planning

3.8 Quick Reference: Micro-Learning Menu

5-Minute Sessions

- Vocabulary flash quiz

- Pronunciation practice

- Quick grammar check

- Daily review

10-Minute Sessions

- Short conversations

- Story summaries

- Opinion sharing

- Problem solving

15-Minute Sessions

- Topic discussions

- Grammar lessons

- Vocabulary building

- Skill practice

20-Minute Sessions

- Mini debates

- Story creation

- Real-world scenarios

- Mixed skill practice

30-Minute Sessions

- Comprehensive practice

- Detailed conversations

- Complex topics

- Progress assessments

Chapter 3 Action Steps

Choose your daily time slot Try one 15-minute session today Set up your tracking system Schedule tomorrow's practice Pick your weekly routine

Chapter Four

Overcoming Common Language Barriers

Chapter Objectives

By the end of this chapter, you will:

- Solve the "no conversation partner" problem with AI

- Break through speaking anxiety using proven techniques

- Practice real-world scenarios before facing them

- Navigate cultural communication challenges confidently

4.1 Barrier #1: "I Have No One to Practice With"

The Isolation Problem

75% of ESL learners report having no regular conversation partner. This creates a vicious cycle:

- No practice → Skills don't improve → Confidence drops → Avoid speaking → No practice

Real Success Story: Ahmed from Egypt

Ahmed moved to a small town in Canada where he knew nobody. English classes were 45 minutes away, and he worked nights.

His AI solution: Daily 30-minute conversations with ChatGPT about his work, interests, and daily life.

Results in 60 days:

- Joined a local hiking group

- Started dating (in English!)

- Got promoted at work

- Made his first Canadian friends

AI as Your 24/7 Conversation Partner

Morning Coffee Chat

Good morning! Let's have a casual 10-minute chat over coffee. Ask me about my plans for today, what I'm looking forward to, and what challenges I might face.

Keep it light and friendly like we're old fr
iends.Start by asking how I slept last night.

Lunch Break Socializing

I'm on my lunch break and want to practice social conversation. Let's chat about
topics people discuss during lunch - weekend plans, current events, hobbies, or
funny stories. Make it feel natural and r
elaxed.Ask me about the most interesting
thing that happened to me this week.

Evening Wind-Down Talk

It's evening and I want to practice re-
flective conversation. Ask me about my
day, what went well, what was challenging, and what I learned. Help me express
my thoughts and feelings clearly.Start by
asking about the best part of my day.

4.2 Barrier #2: Breaking Through Speaking Anxiety

The Fear That Paralyzes

Speaking anxiety affects 89% of ESL learners. Common fears include:

- Making grammar mistakes

- Not finding the right words

- Having an accent

- Being judged or misunderstood

Real Success Story: Sofia from Brazil

Sofia understood English perfectly but hadn't spoken aloud in 3 years. She was terrified of her accent and making mistakes.

Her breakthrough method: Started with ChatGPT voice conversations alone in her room, gradually building confidence.

Results: Now gives weekly presentations at her marketing job.

Progressive Confidence Building

Level 1: Safe Space Practice

> I have speaking anxiety and need to start very slowly. Let's have a conversation where you're extra encouraging and patient. If I make mistakes, correct them very gently. Focus on building my confidence rather than perfect grammar. Let's start by talking about something I love - my favorite food.

Level 2: Mistake Normalization

I'm working on accepting that mistakes
are normal when learning. Let's have a
conversation where you point out that
even native speakers make mistakes sometimes. Help me see errors as learning opportunities, not failures.Let's discuss a
topic I find challenging - explaining my
job duties.

Level 3: Real-World Preparation

I want to practice conversations I might
have in real life, but in a safe environment
first. Help me rehearse [specific scenario]
until I feel confident. Give me multiple
ways to express the same ideas.Scenario:
Asking for help at a store when I can't find
something.

Level 4: Confidence Celebration

Let's have a conversation where you help
me recognize how much my English has

improved. Ask me to tell you about my progress and celebrate my achievements with me.Ask me about the English challenges I've overcome recently.

4.3 Barrier #3: Lack of Real-World Practice Scenarios

The Lab vs. Life Gap

Classroom English often doesn't match real-world situations. You learn to say "How are you?" but not "My internet is down and I need technical support."

Real-World Scenario Bank

Professional Situations

Job Interview Practice

Let's simulate a job interview for [your field]. You be the interviewer and ask me typical questions. Help me answer professionally and give me feedback on my responses. Practice until I feel confiden t.Position: Software DeveloperCompany: Tech startup

Meeting Participation

Simulate a work meeting where I need to contribute ideas. Help me practice expressing opinions, asking questions, and disagreeing politely. Teach me professional phrases for meetings.Meeting topic: Planning the company holiday party

Client Presentation

I need to practice presenting to clients. Help me rehearse explaining [topic] clearly and answering potential questions. Focus on confidence and clarity.Presentation topic: Monthly sales results

Daily Life Situations

Medical Appointments

Let's practice a doctor's appointment. You be the doctor and help me describe symptoms, ask questions, and understand medical advice. This is important for my health and safety.Scenario: I have a persistent headache and back pain

Banking and Finance

Help me practice banking conversations. Simulate opening an account, discussing loans, or resolving account problems. Teach me financial vocabulary I'll actually use.Scenario: I want to open a savings account and ask about interest rates

Emergency Situations

Practice emergency scenarios where clear communication is critical. Help me learn key phrases and stay calm while explaining problems clearly.Scenario: My car broke down and I need to call for help

Social Situations

Making Friends

Help me practice making friends and small talk. Simulate meeting new people at social events and teach me how to keep conversations going naturally.Scenario: First day at a new hobby class (cooking/dancing/sports)

Dating Conversations

Practice casual dating conversations. Help me talk about myself, ask good questions, and handle awkward moments gracefully

.Scenario: Coffee date with someone I met online

Neighbor Interactions

Practice being a good neighbor. Help me with conversations about shared spaces, noise issues, borrowing things, and building community relationships.Scenario : New neighbor introduction and discussing parking

4.4 Barrier #4: Cultural Communication Challenges

Beyond Language: Understanding Culture

Language is only part of communication. Cultural differences in directness, politeness, humor, and social norms can cause misunderstandings.

Cultural Navigation Practice

Understanding Directness Levels

Help me understand when to be direct vs. indirect in English-speaking cultures. Give me examples of the same message expressed in different levels of politeness for different situations.Situation: I need to tell my roommate to clean up after themselves

Workplace Culture

Teach me unwritten rules about workplace communication in [country]. What's considered professional? How do people express disagreement? What topics should I avoid?Focus on: Email etiquette and meeting behavior

Social Etiquette

Help me understand social rules that aren't obvious to non-native speakers. What's considered rude or polite? How do people make and decline invitations?Topic: Dinner party invitations and gift-giving customs

4.5 Building Your AI Practice Network

Creating Conversation Variety

Don't just have one type of conversation. Practice different styles:

Formal Practice Partner

Today you're my formal conversation partner. Speak professionally and help me practice business English, academic discussions, or official situations.Today's focus: Networking at a professional conference

Casual Friend Simulator

Be my casual friend today. Use relaxed language, share opinions, tell jokes, and help me practice informal English I'd use with peers.Today's focus: Discussing weekend plans and funny stories

Supportive Mentor

Act as a supportive mentor who helps me work through language challenges. Be encouraging, patient, and focused on my growth and confidence.Today's focus:

> Preparing for a difficult conversation with my boss

Cultural Guide

> Be my cultural guide today. Help me understand not just the language, but the cultural context behind expressions, customs, and social expectations.Today's focus: Understanding American humor and sarcasm

4.6 Progress Tracking for Barrier Breaking

Weekly Barrier Assessment

Rate your comfort level (1-10) for each area:
Finding Conversation Opportunities: ____**Speaking Without Anxiety:**
____**Handling Real-World Situations:** ____**Understanding Cultural Context:** ____

Monthly Breakthrough Tracker

This month I successfully:
- Spoke in a new situation: _____

- Overcame a specific fear: _____

- Learned a cultural insight: _____

- Gained confidence in: _____

Real-World Application Log

Date: _____ **Situation:** _____**How AI practice helped:** _____**What I'll practice more:** _____

4.7 Emergency Language Toolkit

When You're Stuck in Real Conversations

Buying Time Phrases:
- "Let me think about that for a moment..."

- "That's an interesting question..."

- "Could you repeat that, please?"

Clarification Requests:
- "I want to make sure I understand..."

- "Do you mean...?"

- "Could you explain that differently?"

Polite Problem-Solving:
- "I'm having trouble expressing this in English..."

- "Bear with me while I find the right words..."

- "My English isn't perfect, but I'll try to explain..."

Post-Conversation AI Debrief

> I just had a real conversation in English and want to improve for next time. Help me analyze what went well and what I can practice. Ask me specific questions about the interaction.The conversation was about: [topic]It was with: [context - coworker, stranger, friend, etc.]I felt: [confident, nervous, confused, etc.]

Chapter 4 Action Steps

Identify your biggest language barrier Try one real-world scenario practice Practice with different AI "personality" types Complete a barrier assessment Plan this week's scenario practices Set up your progress tracking system

Chapter Five

AI-Powered Vocabulary and Grammar Building

Chapter Objectives

By the end of this chapter, you will:

- Build vocabulary 3x faster using AI-powered techniques

- Master grammar through contextual practice, not memorization

- Create personalized word lists for your specific needs

- Track vocabulary and grammar progress systematically

5.1 The Vocabulary Explosion Method

Real Success Story: Lin from China

Lin was stuck at intermediate level for 2 years. She knew basic vocabulary but couldn't express complex ideas at work.

Her AI breakthrough: Instead of memorizing random word lists, she used ChatGPT to learn words in context for her specific job in marketing.

Results in 90 days:

- Vocabulary increased from 3,000 to 5,500 words

- Started writing marketing copy in English

- Led client presentations with confidence

- Promoted to senior marketing specialist

The Context-First Approach

Traditional method: Memorize "facilitate" = "to make easier"**AI method:** Learn "facilitate" by using it in 10 different work scenarios

Vocabulary Builder #1: Job-Specific Words

I work as a [your job] and want to learn vocabulary specifically for my field. Give me 10 useful words related to my job, but don't just give definitions. For each word:1. Show me how it's used in my work context2. Give me a sentence I might actually say3. Ask me to use it in my own sentenceMy job: Customer service representative

Vocabulary Builder #2: Interest-Based Learning

I'm passionate about [your hobby/inter-
est] and want to learn vocabulary related
to it. This will help me discuss topics I
care about. Give me words I'd use when
talking about this interest with native s
peakers.My interest: Cooking and trying
new recipes

Vocabulary Builder #3: Daily Life Vocabulary

Help me learn words for everyday situations I encounter regularly. Focus on
practical vocabulary that will improve my
daily communication immediately.Situa
tions I face daily: Commuting, shopping,
talking to neighbors, using technology

5.2 The Grammar Revolution: Context Over Rules

Why Traditional Grammar Teaching Fails

- Focus on rules instead of usage

- Abstract examples instead of personal context

- Memorization instead of practice

- Correction without explanation

The AI Grammar Method

Learn grammar by using it in situations that matter to YOU.

Grammar in Action #1: Tense Mastery

> I struggle with [specific tense]. Instead of explaining rules, help me practice using it in real situations from my life. Give me scenarios where I'd naturally use this tense, then help me practice.Tense focus: Present perfect vs. simple pastMy real situations: Talking about my work experience, travel, achievements

Grammar in Action #2: Complex Sentence Building

> I want to express complex ideas but my sentences are too simple. Help me practice building sophisticated sentences about topics I care about. Show me how to combine ideas smoothly.Topics I want to discuss: My opinions about technology, my career goals, my cultural observations

Grammar in Action #3: Professional Communication

Help me master professional grammar for work situations. Focus on email writing, meeting language, and presentation grammar. Use examples from my actual work context.Work context: Software development team meetings and client communications

5.3 Personalized Learning Systems

Creating Your Personal Word Bank

High-Impact Vocabulary Identifier

Analyze my English level and help me identify 50 high-impact words that would most improve my communication. Focus on words that:1. I'll use frequently2. Make me sound more fluent3. Help express complex ideas4. Are appropriate for my goalsMy level: IntermediateMy goals: Professional advancement and social confidence

Weakness Spotter

> I'll write a paragraph about [topic], and you identify vocabulary gaps where better word choices would improve my expression. Then teach me those better words in context.Topic: Describing my ideal job and career goals

Industry Language Accelerator

> I need to quickly learn the language used in [industry/field]. Help me master key terms, phrases, and communication styles specific to this area.Industry: Healthcare administrationFocus: Patient communication and medical terminology

5.4 Advanced Vocabulary Techniques

The Word Family Method

Root Word Expansion

Take the root word [word] and teach me its entire family - different forms, prefixes, suffixes, and related words. Show me how each form is used in real sentences.Root word: "communicate"Expected family: communication, communicative, communicator, miscommunicate, etc.

Synonym Sophistication

I overuse basic words like "good," "bad," "big," and "small." For each basic word I give you, teach me 5 more sophisticated alternatives and show me when to use each one.Basic words I overuse: nice, interesting, important, difficult

Collocations Master

Teach me natural word combinations (collocations) for [topic]. Native speakers don't just know individual words - they know which words naturally go together.Topic: Business presentationsExample: "make a presentation" not "do a presentation"

The Grammar Automation System

Mistake Pattern Breaker

I consistently make these grammar mistakes: [list your common errors]. For each mistake, give me 10 practice sentences where I have to choose the correct form. Explain why the correct answer is right.My common mistakes:- Articles (a, an, the)- Prepositions (in, on, at)- Verb tenses in storytelling

Fluency Builder

Help me practice grammar that makes speech flow naturally - linking words, transition phrases, and sentence connectors. Focus on making my English sound less choppy and more fluent.Situations: Telling stories, explaining processes, giving opinions

5.5 Rapid Retention Techniques

The Memory Palace Method with AI

Story-Based Learning

> Turn new vocabulary into memorable stories. Take these 10 words [list] and create a connected story that helps me remember their meanings and usage.Word s: negotiate, compromise, deadline, stakeholder, milestone, objective, strategy, implement, evaluate, outcome

Personal Connection Builder

> For each new word I learn, help me create a personal connection or memory that makes it stick. Ask me about my experiences and link new vocabulary to my life. New words: ambitious, resilient, collaborative, innovative, meticulous

Spaced Repetition with Context

Weekly Review System

It's been a week since I learned these words: [list]. Test my retention by asking me to use each word in a new sentence related to current events or recent experiences.Words from last week: [your list]

Progressive Difficulty

I learned the word [word] last week. Now give me increasingly challenging ways to use it - from simple sentences to complex ideas to creative expressions.Target word: "appreciate" (meaning to understand the value of something)

5.6 Tracking Your Language Growth

Vocabulary Progress Tracker

Weekly Vocabulary Log:
- **New words learned:** _____

- **Words successfully used in conversation:** _____

- **Words that need more practice:** _____

- **Favorite new word this week:** _____

Monthly Vocabulary Assessment:

> Test my vocabulary growth from last month. Give me scenarios where I need to use words I've learned recently. Evaluate my progress and suggest focus areas for next month.This month's focus was: Professional presentation vocabulary

Grammar Confidence Meter

Before/After Grammar Check:

> I want to see my grammar improvement. I'll write about [topic] using grammar structures I've been practicing. Compare this to my writing from [time period] ago and show me my progress.Topic: Describing my career goals and challenges comparison period: 1 month ago

Real-World Application Tracker

Date: _____ Situation: _____New vocabulary used successfully: _____Grammar structures practiced: _____Confidence level (1-10): _____

5.7 Common Learning Accelerators

The Explanation Test

The best way to learn vocabulary is to teach it. Ask me to explain these new words to you as if you don't know them. This will show if I truly understand their meaning and usage.Words to explain: sustainable, comprehensive, preliminary, substantial, coherent

The Context Switch Challenge

I learned the word [word] in one context. Now help me use it in completely different contexts to deepen my understanding and flexibility.Word: "execute" Original context: Business (execute a plan)New contexts: Sports, cooking, art, technology

The Precision Practice

Help me move from "good enough" to precise word choice. I'll describe situations using basic vocabulary, and you help me upgrade to more exact and sophisticated words.Situation to describe: A challenging project at work that turned out well

5.8 Grammar Troubleshooting Guide

Problem: "I know the rule but can't use it naturally"

I understand [grammar rule] in theory but struggle to use it in real conversation. Create natural conversation scenarios where I must use this grammar point repeatedly until it becomes automatic.Grammar focus: Conditional sentences (if/when/unless)Real situations: Making plans, discussing possibilities, problem-solving

Problem: "I mix up similar grammar structures"

I confuse [structure A] and [structure B]. Give me pairs of sentences that show the clear difference, then quiz me until I can distinguish them automatically.Confusion: "I have been working" vs "I have worked"

Problem: "My grammar is correct but sounds unnatural"

> My grammar is technically correct but doesn't sound like a native speaker. Help me learn the natural rhythms and patterns that make English flow smoothly.Focus : Making my speech sound more natural and less textbook-like

Chapter 5 Action Steps

Identify your vocabulary learning priority (job, interests, or daily life) Try one vocabulary builder technique Practice one grammar structure in real context Set up your progress tracking system Create your personal word bank for this week Schedule daily vocabulary practice time

Make a Difference with Your Review

Unlock the Power of Generosity

"The best way to find yourself is to lose yourself in the service of others." – Mahatma Gandhi

You've made it halfway through **English Fluency with ChatGPT**—great job!

Would you help someone just like you—excited to improve their English but not sure where to start?

My mission is to make learning English with ChatGPT simple, fun, and confidence-building. But to reach more learners, I need your help.

Most people read reviews before choosing a book. Your words could inspire another learner to begin. Your review could help...

- one more learner speak with confidence at work.

- one more student pass their English exam.

- one more professional share ideas in meetings.

- one more person feel proud of their English journey.

To make a difference, simply scan the QR code or click below:
https://www.amazon.com/review/create-review/?ie=UTF8&channel=glance-detail&asin=1969113022

Thank you from the bottom of my heart!

— *Sawsan Charif*

Chapter Six

Writing with Confidence

Chapter Objectives

By the end of this chapter, you will:

- Write clear, professional emails and documents using AI assistance

- Overcome writing anxiety and perfectionism

- Master different writing styles for various situations

- Edit and improve your writing systematically

6.1 From Blank Page Terror to Writing Confidence

Real Success Story: Priya from India

Priya, a talented engineer, was passed over for promotions because her written communication was unclear. She spent hours on simple emails, paralyzed by fear of making mistakes.

Her AI transformation: Used ChatGPT as a writing coach and editor, practicing daily with real work scenarios.

Results in 8 weeks:

- Writing time reduced from 2 hours to 20 minutes per email

- Started writing technical documentation

- Led written project proposals

- Promoted to team lead

Her secret: Stopped trying to write perfectly the first time. Used AI to iterate and improve.

The Writing Confidence Formula

1. **Brain dump** → Get ideas out without judgment

2. **AI structure** → Organize thoughts logically

3. **Refine** → Improve clarity and flow

4. **Polish** → Perfect grammar and style

6.2 Email Mastery: Professional Communication

The Email That Gets Results

Professional Email Builder

Help me write a professional email for this situation: [describe situation]. Guide me through:

1. Appropriate subject line

2. Professional greeting

3. Clear main message

4. Specific action needed

5. Professional closing

Situation: Requesting a meeting with my manager to discuss a project delay

Difficult Conversation Email

I need to write a sensitive email about [situation]. Help me communicate clearly while remaining professional and diplomatic. The goal is to [desired outcome].

Situation: Explaining why a project deadline cannot be met desired **outcome:** Get deadline extension without damaging relationships

Follow-Up Email Formatter

Help me write a follow-up email that's persistent but not annoying. I need to [purpose] and it's been [time period] since my last contact.

Purpose: Follow up on job application time **since last contact:** 2 weeks

Email Templates for Common Situations

Meeting Request Email

Create an email template for requesting meetings. Include options for:

- Urgent vs. routine meetings

- In-person vs. virtual meetings

- Meeting with superiors vs. peers

- Internal vs. external meetings

I'll customize it for my specific needs.

Project Update Email

Help me create a clear project update email template that includes:

- Progress summary

- Current challenges

- Next steps

- Support needed

- Timeline updates

This is for weekly updates to my team and manager.

6.3 Business Writing That Impresses

Reports and Proposals

Executive Summary Creator

I need to write an executive summary for [topic]. Help me create a compelling one-page summary that busy executives will actually read and understand quickly.

Topic: Proposal to implement new customer service software

Audience: Senior management team

Key goal: Get approval for $50,000 budget

Project Proposal Structure

Guide me through writing a project proposal for [project]. Help me structure it professionally and persuasively, focusing on business benefits and clear next steps.

Project: Creating a mentorship program for new employees

Goal: Reduce turnover and improve job satisfaction

Professional Documentation

Process Documentation Writer

Help me document a work process so clearly that anyone could follow it. Focus on step-by-step clarity and anticipating questions people might have.

Process to document: How to handle customer complaints in our system

Audience: New customer service representatives

Technical Writing Simplifier

I need to explain technical concepts to non-technical people. Help me write clearly about [topic] using simple language and helpful analogies.

Topic: How our new database security system works

Audience: Marketing and sales teams who need to understand basic security protocols

6.4 Academic and Formal Writing

Essay and Report Writing

Thesis Statement Developer

Help me create a strong thesis statement for [topic]. Guide me through developing a clear argument that I can support with evidence throughout my essay.

Topic: The impact of remote work on employee productivity

Type: Argumentative essay for business communication class

Paragraph Structure Master

Teach me to write strong paragraphs using the format you recommend. Take my main idea about [topic] and help me develop it into a well-structured paragraph with clear evidence and analysis.

Main idea: Social media has changed how businesses communicate with customers

Research and Citation Support

Source Integration Helper

I have information from [number] sources about [topic]. Help me integrate these sources smoothly into my writing, using proper transitions and maintaining my own voice.

Topic: Benefits of bilingual education

Sources: 3 academic studies, 2 expert interviews, 1 government report

6.5 Creative and Personal Writing

Storytelling for Professional Impact

Compelling Story Builder

Help me turn this experience into a compelling story I can use in [context]. Focus on clear narrative structure and the lesson or insight that makes it relevant.

Experience: A time when I solved a difficult problem at work through team-work

Context: Job interview behavioral questions

Personal Statement Crafter

Help me write a personal statement for [purpose]. Guide me through highlighting my strengths and experiences in a way that's compelling but not boastful.

Purpose: Graduate school application

Program: MBA with focus on international business

Social Media and Online Presence

Professional Profile Writer

Help me write a professional bio for [platform] that showcases my expertise while being engaging and personable. Focus on my background in [field] and my goals.

Platform: LinkedIn

Field: Digital marketing

Goals: Attract consulting opportunities and network with industry leaders

6.6 Overcoming Writing Anxiety and Perfectionism

The Fear Breakers

Stream of Consciousness Starter

I'm stuck and afraid to start writing about [topic]. Help me do a stream-of-consciousness exercise where I just get my thoughts out without worrying about grammar or structure. Then we'll organize it together.

Topic: My career goals and how this position fits them

Perfectionism Buster

I'm paralyzed by wanting my writing to be perfect. Help me focus on "good enough to communicate clearly" rather than perfection. Give me permission to write a rough draft we can improve together.

Writing task: Cover letter for a job I really want

Confidence Building Exercises

Small Wins Creator

Give me a very simple writing task I can complete successfully in 10 minutes. I need to build confidence with small victories before tackling bigger projects.
Current confidence level: Very low
Areas I'm comfortable with: Describing my daily routine, talking about my hobbies

Progress Celebrator

Compare this writing sample to something I wrote [time period] ago. Help me see the improvements I've made and celebrate my progress.
Current writing: [paste recent writing]
Comparison period: 2 months ago
Focus: Grammar, clarity, confidence

6.7 AI-Powered Editing and Revision

Systematic Improvement Process

Clarity Enhancer

Read this draft and help me make it clearer. Identify sentences that are confusing, ideas that need better explanation, and words that could be more precise.
Draft topic: Explaining why our team needs additional resources

Goal: Convince management to approve hiring two more people

Flow and Structure Optimizer

This writing jumps around too much. Help me reorganize it for better logical flow. Suggest transitions and restructuring to make it easier to follow.

Writing type: Project proposal

Main problem: Ideas are good but poorly organized

Tone Adjuster

Help me adjust the tone of this writing for [audience]. Currently it sounds too [current tone], but it should sound [desired tone].

Current tone: Too casual

Desired tone: Professional but friendly

Audience: Potential clients

Grammar and Style Polishing

Grammar Detective

Be my grammar detective. Find errors in this writing and explain each correction so I can learn to avoid these mistakes in the future.

Focus areas where I struggle: Articles (a, an, the), prepositions, verb tenses

Style Consistency Checker

Check this document for consistency in style, formatting, and voice. Point out where I switch between formal and informal language inappropriately.

Document type: Business proposal

Length: 5 pages

Audience: Corporate clients

6.8 Writing for Different Platforms and Purposes

Digital Communication

Social Media Post Optimizer

Help me write engaging social media posts about [topic] for [platform]. Focus on appropriate length, tone, and hashtag strategy.

Topic: Sharing a professional achievement

Platform: LinkedIn

Goal: Build professional network and credibility

Website Content Creator

Help me write compelling website copy for [page type]. Focus on clear value proposition and call-to-action.

Page type: About page for freelance consulting business

Service: Cross-cultural business communication training

Target audience: International companies

Academic and Professional Growth

Conference Abstract Writer

Help me write an abstract for a conference presentation about [topic]. Include clear research question, methodology, key findings, and significance.

Topic: Impact of AI tools on language learning outcomes

Conference: International Language Education Conference

Length limit: 250 words

6.9 Building Your Writing Routine

Daily Writing Practice

Morning Pages with AI

Let's do a morning writing exercise. Give me a prompt to write about for 10 minutes, then help me extract one useful insight or idea from what I wrote.

Today's focus: Professional development goals

Writing Challenge Generator

Give me a daily writing challenge that will improve a specific skill. Make it achievable in 15-20 minutes but meaningful for my growth.

Skill to improve: Writing persuasive arguments

Current level: Can state opinions but struggle to support them convincingly

Progress Tracking

Writing Skills Assessment

Evaluate my writing in these areas and give me a score (1-10) for each:

- Clarity of ideas

- Grammar accuracy

- Professional tone

- Logical organization

- Engagement level

Based on this writing sample: [paste sample]

Chapter 6 Action Steps

Write one professional email using AI guidance

Try the brain dump → structure → refine process

Practice editing a piece of your writing with AI help

Set up a daily writing routine (even 10 minutes)

Identify your biggest writing challenge and create a practice plan

Track your writing confidence level (1-10) for comparison later

Chapter Seven

Speaking Fluency and Pronunciation

Chapter Objectives

By the end of this chapter, you will:

- Overcome speaking anxiety and build confident conversation skills

- Master pronunciation of difficult sounds and words

- Practice real-world speaking scenarios with AI feedback

- Develop fluency through structured speaking exercises

- Learn accent reduction and clarity improvement techniques

7.1 From Silent to Confident Speaker

Real Success Story: Ahmed from Egypt

Ahmed was brilliant in written English but froze during presentations and meetings. His fear of mispronunciation kept him silent in important discussions, limiting his career growth.

His AI transformation: Used voice AI tools and conversation practice with ChatGPT to build speaking confidence systematically.

Results in 12 weeks:

- Led his first team presentation successfully

- Started participating actively in international video calls

- Received positive feedback on his communication clarity

- Got promoted to client-facing role

His secret: Practiced speaking alone with AI feedback before real conversations, building confidence in a safe environment.

The Speaking Confidence Formula

1. **Practice privately** → Build skills without judgment

2. **Get AI feedback** → Identify specific areas to improve

3. **Simulate real scenarios** → Practice actual situations you'll face

4. **Apply gradually** → Use new skills in low-stakes real conversations

5. **Iterate and improve** → Continuous refinement

7.2 Pronunciation Mastery with AI

Difficult Sound Training

Pronunciation Coach

I struggle with pronouncing [specific sounds/words]. Act as my pronunciation coach and help me practice these systematically. Give me:

1. Clear explanation of tongue and mouth positioning

2. Similar words to practice the same sound

3. Sentences that use these sounds repeatedly

4. Tips for remembering the correct pronunciation

Sounds I struggle with: TH sounds (think, this, that)**My native language:** Spanish

Word Stress Patterns

Help me understand and practice word stress patterns in English. Focus on [word type] and give me exercises to master the rhythm.

Word type: Three-syllable words ending in -tion (education, information, communication)**Goal:** Sound more natural and easier to understand

Minimal Pairs Practice

Create minimal pairs exercises for sounds I confuse. Give me word pairs that differ only in [target sounds] and sentences to practice them.

Target sounds: /b/ vs /v/ (berry vs very, boat vs vote)**Practice level:** Intermediate

Connected Speech and Rhythm

Natural Speech Flow Trainer

Help me practice connected speech patterns like linking, reduction, and contractions. Focus on common phrases I use in [context].

Context: Business meetings and presentations

Goal: Sound more fluent and natural, less robotic

Rhythm and Intonation Coach

Teach me English rhythm and intonation patterns. Help me practice with sentences that show [emotion/purpose].

Emotion/Purpose: Asking questions politely, showing enthusiasm, disagreeing diplomatically

Current problem: My speech sounds flat and monotone

7.3 Conversation Skills Development

Real-World Scenario Practice

Job Interview Simulator

Let's practice a job interview conversation. You ask me typical questions for [position type], and I'll respond. Give me feedback on:

- Clarity of my answers

- Professional language use

- Confidence level

- Areas for improvement

Position type: Software project manager
Company type: International tech startup

Small Talk Master

Help me practice small talk conversations for [context]. Give me natural conversation starters and teach me how to keep conversations flowing smoothly.
   Context: Networking events and office break room conversations
   Goal: Build relationships with colleagues and new contacts

Difficult Conversation Practice

Let's role-play a challenging conversation where I need to [objective]. You play the other person, and help me practice diplomatic language and confident delivery.
   Objective: Ask my manager for a raise and promotion
   Challenge: Manager is very busy and direct, doesn't like long explanations

Presentation and Public Speaking

Presentation Skills Trainer

Help me prepare and practice a presentation about [topic]. Guide me through:
   1. Strong opening that captures attention

   2. Clear structure and transitions

3. Engaging delivery techniques

4. Confident closing and Q&A handling

Topic: Quarterly sales results and next quarter goals
Audience: Senior management team (8 people)**Time limit:** 15 minutes

Story Structure for Speaking

Help me structure and practice telling this story/experience for [context]. Make it engaging and relevant to my audience.

Story: How I solved a major technical problem under pressure

Context: Leadership interview question about handling challenges

Goal: Demonstrate problem-solving and leadership skills

7.4 Accent Reduction and Clarity

Targeted Accent Work

Accent Assessment and Plan

Help me identify the strongest features of my [native language] accent that affect my English clarity. Create a personalized improvement plan focusing on the most important changes.

Native language: Mandarin Chinese

English level: Advanced, but accent affects professional communication

Priority: Being understood clearly in business contexts

Vowel Sounds Mastery

My vowel sounds are unclear and confusing to native speakers. Help me practice the English vowel system systematically, starting with [vowel sounds].

Vowel sounds: /æ/ (cat), /ʌ/ (cup), /ɔ:/ (thought) - these don't exist in my language

Current problem: People often ask me to repeat myself

Consonant Clusters Practice

English consonant clusters at the beginning and end of words are difficult for me. Help me practice [specific clusters] with targeted exercises.

Specific clusters: str- (street, strong), -ths (months, lengths), -cts (facts, acts)**Native language background:** Japanese (simpler consonant structure)

Fluency Development Exercises

Spontaneous Speaking Trainer

Give me spontaneous speaking challenges to build fluency. Provide [topic] and time me for [duration]. Then give feedback on fluency, not just accuracy.

Topic type: Current events, personal opinions, hypothetical situations

Duration: 2 minutes without stopping

Goal: Reduce pauses and hesitation

Fluency vs Accuracy Balance

Help me find the right balance between speaking fluently and being grammatically correct. I tend to [current problem] and need practice with natural, confident speech.

Current problem: Stop and self-correct too often, which breaks the flow

Goal: Communicate ideas clearly even if not 100% perfect grammar

7.5 Voice AI Tools and Technology

AI-Powered Speaking Practice

Voice Recording Analysis

I'll record myself speaking about [topic] for [duration]. Help me analyze the recording for:

- Pronunciation issues

- Pace and rhythm

- Confidence level

- Areas needing improvement

Topic: My professional background and career goals

Duration: 3 minutes

Purpose: Preparation for networking events

Shadowing Practice Guide

Help me use shadowing technique with [content type]. Guide me through the process and suggest how to track my progress.

Content type: TED Talks about leadership and innovation

Current level: Can follow about 70% at normal speed

Goal: Improve rhythm, intonation, and connected speech

AI Conversation Partner

Be my conversation partner for regular speaking practice. Today's topic is [topic]. Keep the conversation natural and give me gentle corrections when needed.

Topic: Travel experiences and future travel plans

Style: Casual, friendly conversation between colleagues

Focus: Using past and future tenses naturally

7.6 Building Speaking Confidence

Overcoming Speaking Anxiety

Fear Identification and Solutions

I'm afraid of [specific speaking fear]. Help me understand why this fear exists and create a step-by-step plan to overcome it gradually.

Specific fear: Making grammar mistakes in front of native speakers

Current impact: Avoid speaking up in meetings and social situations

Goal: Speak confidently even if not perfect

Confidence Building Exercises

Give me low-pressure speaking exercises that will build my confidence gradually. Start with [comfort level] and help me progress.

Comfort level: Can read aloud confidently, struggle with spontaneous speech

Practice environment: Alone at home initially

Timeline: 4 weeks to feel ready for real conversations

Positive Self-Talk for Speakers

Help me develop positive self-talk before speaking situations. Replace my negative thoughts with constructive, confidence-building ones.

Negative thoughts: "Everyone will notice my accent," "I'll embarrass myself," "My English isn't good enough"

Target situations: Video calls with international colleagues

Progressive Speaking Challenges

30-Day Speaking Challenge

Create a 30-day speaking improvement challenge with daily tasks that gradually increase in difficulty. Start with [current level].

Current level: Comfortable with prepared topics, nervous with unexpected questions

Goal: Handle spontaneous conversations confidently**Available practice time:** 20 minutes per day

Real-World Application Plan

Help me create a plan to apply my speaking practice in real situations. Suggest low-risk opportunities to practice [target skills].

Target skills: Asking questions in meetings, giving opinions, making small talk

Work environment: International company, mostly video calls**Personality:** Introverted, prefer to prepare before speaking

7.7 Advanced Speaking Techniques

Professional Communication Mastery

Meeting Participation Skills

Help me practice active participation in meetings. Teach me phrases and techniques for:

1. Contributing ideas confidently

2. Asking clarifying questions

3. Politely disagreeing or offering alternatives

4. Following up on action items

Meeting type: Weekly team status meetings
Role: Project coordinator reporting to senior managers

Persuasive Speaking Practice

I need to practice persuasive speaking for [situation]. Help me structure my argument and practice delivering it convincingly.

Situation: Proposing a new workflow process to resistant team members
Challenge: Some team members prefer the current system

Goal: Get buy-in for 3-month trial period

Cross-Cultural Communication

Help me adapt my speaking style for [cultural context]. Teach me appropriate communication norms and practice culturally sensitive language.

Cultural context: Presenting to Japanese business partners

Goal: Show respect while being clear about project requirements

Challenge: Balancing directness with cultural sensitivity

Advanced Fluency Development

Idiomatic Expression Practice

Help me learn and practice using [number] common idioms and expressions naturally in conversation. Focus on [context type].

Number: 10 most useful idioms

Context type: Business and professional settings

Goal: Sound more natural and connect better with native speakers

Sophisticated Vocabulary in Speech

Help me incorporate more sophisticated vocabulary into my spoken English. Practice using [level] vocabulary in casual conversation without sounding artificial.

Level: Advanced academic and professional vocabulary

Current problem: I know these words but only use them in writing

Goal: Sound more educated and articulate when speaking

7.8 Specialized Speaking Contexts

Academic and Professional Presentations

Conference Presentation Prep

Help me prepare for a conference presentation about [topic]. Focus on clear delivery, engaging the audience, and handling Q&A confidently.

Topic: AI applications in language learning

Audience: International educators and researchers

Duration: 20 minutes plus 10 minutes Q&A

Teaching and Training Skills

I need to improve my speaking for teaching/training situations. Help me practice [specific aspect] with clear explanations and engaging delivery.

Specific aspect: Explaining complex technical concepts to beginners

Subject matter: Database management systems

Audience: New employees with no technical background

Social and Cultural Contexts

Social Conversation Mastery

Help me practice social conversations for [setting]. Focus on building connections and maintaining engaging dialogue.

Setting: Company social events and after-work gatherings

Goal: Build better relationships with colleagues

Challenge: Moving beyond work topics to personal connection

Cultural Event Participation

I'll be attending [event type] and want to participate confidently in conversations. Help me prepare appropriate topics and social language.

Event type: Professional networking mixer in the healthcare industry

Role: New member looking to build professional relationships

Goal: Have meaningful conversations with 5+ people

7.9 Creating Your Speaking Practice System

Daily Practice Routine

Speaking Habit Builder

Help me design a daily speaking practice routine that fits my schedule and targets my biggest challenges. I have [time available] and want to focus on [priority areas].

Time available: 15 minutes in the morning, 10 minutes during lunch

Priority areas: Pronunciation clarity, conversation confidence

Current routine: None - need to start from zero

Progress Tracking System

Create a system for tracking my speaking progress. Include metrics for [aspects] and help me set realistic monthly goals.

Aspects: Pronunciation accuracy, fluency, confidence level, vocabulary usage-**Goal timeline:** Significant improvement in 6 months**Current baseline:** [rate current skills 1-10 in each area]

Feedback and Improvement Loop

Self-Assessment Tools

Teach me to evaluate my own speaking objectively. Create checklists and reflection questions for after practice sessions.

  Focus areas: Clarity, pace, confidence, grammar accuracy

  Goal: Become better at identifying what to improve next

Finding Speaking Partners

Help me find and organize speaking practice opportunities with [partner type]. Create conversation topics and structure for productive practice sessions.

  Partner type: Other English learners at similar level

  Meeting frequency: Twice per week, 30 minutes each

  Platform: Video calls (we live in different cities)

Chapter 7 Action Steps

Complete pronunciation assessment and identify top 3 sounds to improve

Practice one conversation scenario using AI feedback

Record yourself speaking for 2 minutes and analyze with AI help

Try one technique for overcoming speaking anxiety

Set up daily speaking practice routine (even 5 minutes)

Find one real-world opportunity to practice this week

Chapter Eight

Real-World Application and Integration

Chapter Objectives

By the end of this chapter, you will:

- Transition from translating to thinking directly in English

- Develop automatic English responses and reactions

- Use AI to accelerate the mental shift to English thinking

- Create an English-dominant mental environment

- Achieve the breakthrough moment where English becomes natural

8.1 The Mental Revolution: From Translation to Direct Thinking

Real Success Story: Maria from Brazil

Maria had been studying English for 8 years but still translated everything in her head. She was fluent on paper but exhausted from constant mental translation during conversations.

Her AI transformation: Used ChatGPT to practice "English thinking" exercises and created an immersive mental environment using AI conversations.

Results in 6 weeks:

- Stopped translating during conversations

- Started dreaming in English regularly

- Response time in conversations improved dramatically

- Felt relaxed and natural speaking English

- Colleagues noticed her newfound fluency and confidence

Her breakthrough moment: The day she caught herself thinking through a work problem entirely in English without realizing it.

The English Thinking Revolution Formula

1. **Interrupt translation habits** → Catch yourself and redirect

2. **Create English mental space** → Dedicated thinking time in English

3. **Use AI for thought practice** → Practice thinking patterns with feedback

4. **Immerse your inner voice** → Replace mental commentary with English

5. **Celebrate small wins** → Notice and reinforce English thinking mo-

ments

8.2 Breaking the Translation Habit

Identifying Translation Patterns

Translation Trap Detector

Help me identify when and why I'm translating instead of thinking directly in English. Analyze my habits in [situation type] and create awareness strategies.

   Situation type: During work meetings when I need to respond quickly

   Current pattern: I form the idea in Portuguese, translate to English, then speak

   Goal: Think the idea directly in English

Mental Speed Booster

I want to increase my mental processing speed in English. Help me practice [skill type] without translation delays.

   Skill type: Responding to unexpected questions and expressing opinions spontaneously

   Current delay: 3-5 seconds while I mentally translate

   Target: Immediate, natural responses

Native Language Interference

My native language [language] interferes with my English thinking in these ways: [interference patterns]. Help me overcome these specific challenges.

Language: Korean

Interference patterns: Word order confusion, honorific system affecting tone choices, difficulty with articles

Priority: Stop restructuring sentences in my head

Direct English Thinking Practice

Stream of Consciousness Training

Let's practice stream of consciousness thinking in English. Give me a topic and I'll think out loud for [duration] without stopping to translate or perfect my grammar.

Topic: My weekend plans and why I'm excited about them

Duration: 3 minutes non-stop

Goal: Train my brain to think directly in English flow

Inner Monologue Replacement

Help me replace my inner monologue with English. Guide me through exercises to narrate my daily activities and thoughts in English instead of [native language].

Native language: French

Current habit: All mental commentary is in French

Target activities: Morning routine, commute, work tasks

Emotional Response Training

I want to have emotional reactions directly in English. Help me practice expressing [emotion types] spontaneously without mental translation.

    Emotion types: Surprise, frustration, excitement, disappointment

    Current problem: Strong emotions trigger native language thinking

    Goal: Natural English emotional expression

8.3 Creating an English Mental Environment

Immersive Thinking Exercises

English-Only Mental Days

Help me plan "English thinking days" where I commit to thinking only in English. Create structure, challenges, and backup strategies for [duration].

    Duration: Starting with 2-hour blocks, building to full days

    Biggest challenge: Automatic native language thoughts during stress

    Support needed: Reminders and mental reset techniques

Problem-Solving in English

Guide me through solving [problem type] entirely in English. Help me think through options, weigh decisions, and reach conclusions without translation.

    Problem type: Planning a career change and evaluating different options

    Goal: Make the entire decision-making process happen in English

    Complexity: Multi-step problem requiring analytical thinking

Creative Thinking Sessions

Let's do creative brainstorming entirely in English. Give me [creative challenge] and help me generate ideas without reverting to my native language.

Creative challenge: Innovative solutions for improving workplace communication

Duration: 20 minutes of pure English creative thinking

Goal: Access creativity directly through English

Mental Habit Reconstruction

English Self-Talk Developer

Help me develop positive English self-talk patterns. Replace my [native language] internal dialogue with encouraging English thoughts.

Native language: Hindi

Current self-talk: Mix of Hindi and English, mostly Hindi during stress

Target areas: Work confidence, social situations, problem-solving

Memory Formation in English

I want to form memories directly in English. Help me practice describing experiences as they happen, creating English memory pathways.

Practice scenario: Describing my workday experience as it unfolds

Goal: Remember events with English thoughts attached, not native language

Timeline: 2 weeks to establish this habit

Decision-Making Process

Guide me through making decisions entirely in English, from considering options to final choice. Practice with [decision type].

Decision type: Choosing between job offers with multiple factors to consider

Current habit: Analyze in native language, then translate conclusions

Goal: Complete decision process in English thinking

8.4 Advanced Mental Fluency Techniques

Unconscious English Processing

Dream Programming

Help me understand and encourage dreaming in English. What techniques can shift my subconscious processing toward English?

Current state: Dreams are 90% in native language

Goal: Increase English dreams and subconscious English processing

Methods: Bedtime routines, visualization, daily practices

Automatic Response Development

I want automatic English responses to common situations. Help me program [response type] until they become unconscious habits.

Response type: Polite greetings, expressing gratitude, asking for clarification

Current problem: Always pause to formulate responses consciously

Goal: Instant, natural reactions

Mental Flexibility Training

Help me develop mental flexibility to switch thinking styles within English for different contexts [context types].

Context types: Casual conversation vs. formal presentation vs. creative brainstorming

Goal: Adjust thinking patterns automatically for different situations

Current limitation: One thinking mode regardless of context

Complex Thought Patterns

Abstract Concept Processing

I struggle thinking about abstract concepts directly in English. Help me practice [concept type] without mental translation.

Concept type: Philosophy, ethics, complex emotions, theoretical ideas

Current pattern: Understand in native language, then translate for expression

Goal: Process abstract thoughts natively in English

Multi-Step Reasoning

Guide me through complex reasoning entirely in English. Practice with [reasoning type] that requires multiple logical steps.

Reasoning type: Analyzing business strategy options with multiple variables

Complexity level: 5-6 step logical progression

Goal: Complete analysis without native language assistance

Cultural Thinking Patterns

Help me adopt English/Western thinking patterns for [cultural context] while maintaining my cultural identity.

Cultural context: Direct communication in business vs. my culture's indirect style

Goal: Think in culturally appropriate English patterns when needed

Balance: Professional effectiveness without losing cultural self

8.5 Accelerated Immersion with AI

AI-Powered Mental Training

Consciousness Stream Partner

Be my thinking partner for stream-of-consciousness practice. Engage with my thoughts in real-time as I process [topic] entirely in English.

Topic: Analyzing my career goals and life priorities

Style: Supportive questioning that keeps me thinking in English

Duration: 15-minute guided thinking session

Mental Challenge Generator

Create daily mental challenges that force English thinking. Design [challenge type] that I can't solve by translating.

Challenge type: Creative problem-solving, wordplay, cultural analysis

Difficulty level: Intermediate to advanced

Goal: Build English thinking strength like mental exercise

Subconscious Programming Assistant

Help me create subconscious programming routines to shift my default thinking language to English. Include [technique types].

Technique types: Visualization, affirmations, bedtime programming, trigger phrases

Target: Unconscious shift to English as primary thinking language

Timeline: 30 days of consistent practice

Real-Time Thinking Support

Live Thinking Coach

Coach me through thinking in English during [real situation]. Provide real-time guidance to prevent translation relapses.

Real situation: Planning a presentation while walking through ideas out loud

Support needed: Catch translation moments, suggest English alternatives

Goal: Complete planning process in English

Mental Block Breaker

When I get stuck thinking in English, help me break through with [breakthrough techniques]. Practice with challenging [topic type].

Breakthrough techniques: Word association, perspective shifting, simplified expression

Topic type: Complex technical explanations or emotional discussions**Current problem:** Revert to native language when ideas get complex

Confidence Reinforcement

Help me build confidence in my English thinking ability. Create [reinforcement type] to strengthen my belief in direct English thought.

Reinforcement type: Success recognition, progress tracking, positive reframing

Current doubt: "My English thinking isn't sophisticated enough"

Goal: Trust my English thinking for all mental tasks

8.6 Measuring the Mental Shift

Progress Tracking Indicators

English Thinking Assessment

Help me assess my current level of English thinking across [domains]. Create benchmarks to track improvement.

Domains: Daily routine thoughts, work problem-solving, emotional processing, creative thinking

Current estimate: 30% English, 70% native language

Goal: 80% English within 3 months

Breakthrough Moment Recognition

Help me recognize and celebrate breakthrough moments in English thinking. What signs indicate I'm making the mental shift?

Areas to monitor: Speed of response, complexity of English thoughts, emotional reactions

Goal: Identify when English becomes my natural thinking mode

Celebration plan: Acknowledge progress to reinforce positive changes

Native Speaker Thinking Comparison

Help me understand how native speakers think in different situations and work toward similar mental patterns in [context types].

Context types: Problem-solving, emotional processing, humor, cultural references

Goal: Think more like a native speaker while maintaining my unique perspective

Method: Analyze thinking patterns and practice similar approaches

Advanced Integration Techniques

Bilingual Advantage Optimization

Help me leverage my bilingual brain for enhanced thinking rather than seeing translation as a weakness. Optimize [advantage types].

Advantage types: Cultural perspective switching, creative problem-solving, flexible thinking

Current view: Bilingualism as obstacle to English fluency

New goal: Bilingual thinking as superpower with English dominance

Professional English Identity

Help me develop a professional English-thinking identity for work contexts. Create mental frameworks for [professional areas].

Professional areas: Leadership, technical communication, client relations, team management

Goal: Professional English persona that thinks natively in business contexts

Current gap: Confident in social English, translate for professional thoughts

Cultural Integration Balance

Help me integrate English thinking while maintaining my cultural thought patterns. Balance [cultural elements] with English fluency.

Cultural elements: Respect patterns, family concepts, spiritual/philosophical frameworks

Goal: Think fluidly in English without losing cultural identity**Challenge:** Some concepts don't translate directly between cultures

8.7 Creating Lasting Mental Changes

Habit Installation Systems

30-Day English Mind Challenge

Create a comprehensive 30-day program to shift my dominant thinking language to English. Include daily [practice types] with increasing difficulty.

Practice types: Mental exercises, real-world applications, progress checkpoints

Current thinking ratio: 25% English, 75% native language

Target ratio: 75% English, 25% native language

Mental Environment Design

Help me redesign my mental environment to support English thinking. Address [environmental factors] that trigger native language thoughts.

Environmental factors: Stress responses, familiar routines, emotional triggers

Goal: Create mental cues that automatically prompt English thinking

Timeline: Sustainable changes within 6 weeks

Long-term Maintenance Plan

Create a long-term plan to maintain English thinking dominance after achieving it. Include [maintenance elements] to prevent regression.

Maintenance elements: Regular challenges, progress monitoring, refresher exercises

Goal: Permanent shift to English as primary thinking language

Concern: Losing progress during stressful periods or long native language exposure

Integration with Daily Life

Workplace English Thinking

Help me establish English thinking in all work-related mental activities. Create systems for [work contexts].

Work contexts: Team meetings, project planning, client communication, problem-solving

Current state: Mix of both languages depending on complexity

Goal: 100% English thinking during work hours

Social Life Integration

Guide me in maintaining English thinking during social activities with [social groups]. Balance social connection with mental practice.

Social groups: Mixed nationality friends, English-speaking colleagues, international community

Challenge: Relaxing into native language with comfortable friends

Goal: Natural English thinking in all social contexts

Personal Life English Mind

Help me extend English thinking into personal life activities like [personal areas] without losing emotional connection.

Personal areas: Family relationships, personal reflection, hobby planning, life decisions

Current pattern: Personal life = native language, professional life = English

Goal: Seamless English thinking across all life areas

8.8 Breakthrough Acceleration Techniques

Intensive Mental Immersion

English Thinking Bootcamp

Design an intensive program to accelerate my mental shift to English. Create [intensity level] challenges for rapid progress.

Intensity level: High-intensity, 2-week focused program

Available time: 2 hours daily dedicated practice

Goal: Breakthrough moment within 2 weeks

Mental Fluency Sprint

Create a 7-day mental fluency sprint focusing on [target area]. Include hourly exercises and real-time challenges.

Target area: Spontaneous opinion formation and expression

Current weakness: Long delays when forming opinions in English

Goal: Instant opinion formation in English

Immersion Simulation

Help me create total English mental immersion without traveling. Design [simulation techniques] for complete mental environment shift.

Simulation techniques: Mental roleplaying, environment modification, social interaction changes

Duration: 5 consecutive days of total English mental immersion

Support system: AI coaching and progress tracking

Expert-Level Mental Processing

Native-Level Thought Complexity

Help me process complex, nuanced thoughts at native speaker level. Practice with [complexity types] that challenge advanced thinking.

Complexity types: Philosophical debates, ethical dilemmas, creative innovation, strategic planning

Current limitation: Simplify thoughts to match English ability

Goal: Full complexity thinking directly in English

Cultural Nuance Integration

Help me think with English cultural nuances and implied meanings. Develop understanding of [cultural thinking patterns].

Cultural thinking patterns: Humor, irony, indirect communication, cultural references

Goal: Understand and think with native cultural frameworks

Application: Better social and professional relationships

Expert Communication Mindset

Develop expert-level English thinking for [expertise area]. Think like a native speaker expert in my field.

Expertise area: Software engineering and team leadership

Goal: Think about technical and leadership challenges with native-level sophistication

Current gap: Can explain but can't think complex technical strategies in English

Chapter 8 Action Steps

Track your thinking language ratio for 3 days (native vs English)

Practice 1 stream-of-consciousness session entirely in English

Replace inner monologue with English for 1 specific daily activity

Attempt to solve 1 real problem entirely through English thinking

Notice and celebrate your first "automatic English thought" moment

Set up environmental cues that trigger English thinking mode

Chapter Nine

Practical AI Tools and Resources

Chapter Objectives

By the end of this chapter, you will:

- Create sustainable systems for lifelong English improvement

- Avoid common plateaus and maintain momentum

- Use AI to continuously challenge yourself at higher levels

- Build an English learning ecosystem that grows with you

- Develop mastery mindset for ongoing excellence

9.1 The Lifelong Learner's Success Story

Real Success Story: David from Germany

David reached "advanced" English after 3 years of AI-powered learning, but then faced a new challenge: How to continue growing when you're already fluent? How to go from good to exceptional?

His Advanced AI Strategy: Created a personalized "English Excellence Ecosystem" using multiple AI tools for different skills, always pushing beyond his comfort zone.

Results after 2 more years:

- Became the go-to English speaker for international projects at his company

- Started a successful YouTube channel in English (50K+ subscribers)

- Got offered positions in London and New York

- Achieved native-level fluency that even surprised native speakers

- Developed expertise in specialized vocabulary for his industry

His Mastery Secret: Never stopped learning. Created systems that automatically introduced new challenges and prevented stagnation.

The Continuous Growth Formula

1. **Never plateau** → Always add new challenges before mastering current level

2. **Systematic expansion** → Deliberately target new skills and contexts

3. **Quality obsession** → Perfect what you have while learning what's next

4. **Adaptive systems** → Change methods as your needs evolve

5. **Teaching others** → Solidify knowledge by helping fellow learners

9.2 Anti-Plateau Systems

Identifying and Breaking Plateaus

Plateau Detection AI

Help me identify if I'm in a plateau and what type. Analyze my recent progress in [skill areas] and detect stagnation patterns.

Skill areas: Vocabulary expansion, conversation fluency, professional writing, cultural understanding

Time period: Last 3 months of practice

Warning signs: Feeling comfortable, same types of mistakes, avoiding challenges

Plateau-Breaking Challenge Creator

I think I'm plateauing in [specific area]. Create a 2-week intensive challenge to break through to the next level.

Specific area: Advanced conversation skills - I can handle routine topics but struggle with abstract discussions

Current comfort zone: Work topics, daily life, basic opinions

Target breakthrough: Philosophy, complex social issues, nuanced cultural topics

Skill Gap Identifier

Analyze my current English abilities and identify hidden gaps that prevent me from reaching the next level. Focus on [mastery area].

Mastery area: Professional communication and leadership presence

Current level: Strong technical communication, weaker in influence and persuasion

Goal: C2-level professional influence in English

Advanced Challenge Systems

Monthly Mastery Projects

Design monthly projects that push me beyond my current abilities. This month's focus: [skill type] with [complexity level].

Skill type: Advanced writing and thought leadership

Complexity level: Writing articles that could be published in industry magazines

Timeline: 4 weeks to complete research, writing, and refinement

Comfort Zone Expander

Help me systematically expand my English comfort zone. Design weekly challenges that feel slightly difficult but achievable in [context areas].

Context areas: Public speaking, debate, creative writing, technical training

Current comfort: 7/10 difficulty level

Target expansion: Regular practice at 8.5/10 difficulty

Skill Integration Challenges

Create challenges that combine multiple English skills simultaneously. Practice [skill combination] in realistic scenarios.

Skill combination: Listening + critical thinking + persuasive speaking + cultural sensitivity

Scenario type: International business negotiations and conflict resolution

Goal: Seamless integration of all advanced skills

9.3 Advanced AI Learning Partnerships

Specialized AI Tutoring

Expert-Level Conversation Partner

Be my advanced conversation partner for [expertise topic]. Challenge me with native-level discussions and expert terminology.

Expertise topic: Artificial intelligence and machine learning trends

Discussion level: PhD/professional researcher level

Goal: Discuss cutting-edge concepts with complete fluency and confidence

Cultural Immersion Simulator

Create deep cultural immersion experiences focused on [cultural aspect]. Help me understand and navigate complex cultural nuances.

Cultural aspect: American business culture and unwritten rules

Focus areas: Office politics, networking strategies, leadership styles

Goal: Cultural fluency that matches language fluency

Industry-Specific Language Coach

Help me master the specialized language of [industry] at native professional level. Include jargon, cultural references, and communication styles.

Industry: International finance and investment banking

Current level: General business English

Target: Sound like a native speaker working in Wall Street

Continuous Challenge Generation

Weekly Skill Rotation

Create a rotating weekly system that continuously challenges different aspects of my English. Design [rotation type] for sustained growth.

Rotation type: 4-week cycles covering speaking, writing, listening, cultural competence

Intensity: Each week should feel challenging but not overwhelming

Integration: Skills should build on each other across the cycle

Adaptive Difficulty System

Create an adaptive system that automatically increases difficulty as I improve. Design [progression type] that prevents plateaus.

Progression type: Vocabulary complexity, topic sophistication, time pressure, multitasking demands

Current baseline: Handle most topics comfortably with preparation time

Adaptation trigger: When success rate exceeds 85% for 2 weeks

Real-World Mission Generator

Give me real-world missions that require English skills beyond my current comfort zone. This week's mission: [mission type].

Mission type: Lead a cross-cultural team project with stakeholders from 5 countries

Skills required: Diplomacy, technical explanation, conflict resolution, cultural bridge-building

Success metric: Project completion with positive feedback from all stakeholders

9.4 Building Your English Ecosystem

Comprehensive Growth Environment

Personal Learning Ecosystem Designer

Help me design a complete English learning ecosystem that grows with me. Include [ecosystem components] for sustainable long-term development.

Ecosystem components: AI tools, human partners, content sources, practice opportunities, feedback systems

Current level: Advanced intermediate

Goal: System that automatically provides appropriate challenges as I advance

English Identity Development

Help me develop a sophisticated English-speaking identity that feels authentic and powerful. Focus on [identity aspects].

Identity aspects: Professional presence, social confidence, cultural adaptability, thought leadership

Current challenge: Still feel like "translator" rather than "native thinker"

Goal: Authentic English self that feels natural and confident

Opportunity Creation System

Help me create systems that generate real opportunities to use advanced English skills. Design [opportunity types] that match my goals.

Opportunity types: Speaking engagements, writing publications, mentoring roles, international projects

Current situation: Limited high-level English practice opportunities

Goal: Regular high-stakes English usage that drives improvement

Community and Network Building

English Excellence Network

Help me build a network of advanced English learners and native speakers for mutual growth. Design [network strategy] for long-term relationships.

Network strategy: Online communities, local meetups, professional associations, mentorship exchanges

Target connections: People who challenge and inspire my English development

Goal: Sustainable community that supports lifelong learning

Teaching and Mentoring Setup

Help me start teaching/mentoring other English learners to solidify my own skills. Create [teaching approach] that benefits everyone.

Teaching approach: Peer tutoring, online content creation, workshop facilitation

My strengths: Grammar, writing, AI-powered learning methods

Goal: Teaching that deepens my own understanding while helping others

Professional English Brand

Help me build a professional brand around my English communication skills. Develop [brand strategy] for career advancement.

Brand strategy: Thought leadership, cross-cultural expertise, communication coaching

Platform focus: LinkedIn, industry conferences, company leadership roles

Goal: Recognition as exceptional English communicator in my field

9.5 Specialized Mastery Tracks

Choose Your Mastery Path

Academic Excellence Track

I want to achieve academic-level English mastery. Design a progression path for [academic focus] that reaches PhD-level communication.

Academic focus: Research writing, conference presentations, peer review participation

Current level: Can read academic papers, struggle with sophisticated writing

Timeline: 18 months to academic English mastery

Business Leadership Track

Create a business leadership English development path. Focus on [leadership aspects] for international executive presence.

Leadership aspects: Strategic communication, stakeholder management, cultural leadership, crisis communication

Goal position: VP-level international role requiring exceptional communication

Current gap: Technical skills strong, leadership presence needs development

Creative Expression Track

Help me develop creative English abilities for [creative focus]. Build skills for artistic and innovative expression.

Creative focus: Creative writing, storytelling, humor, wordplay, cultural commentary

Current creativity: Limited to functional communication

Goal: Express complex emotions and ideas creatively in English

Cultural Bridge-Builder Track

Develop my English for cross-cultural leadership and bridge-building. Focus on [cultural competencies].

Cultural competencies: Multicultural team leadership, diplomatic communication, cultural translation, conflict resolution

Background: Native culture + English fluency = unique bridge-building potential

Goal: Recognized expert in cross-cultural communication

Advanced Skill Development

Mastery-Level Speaking Skills

Help me achieve mastery-level speaking abilities in [speaking contexts]. Design intensive training for native-level presentation.

Speaking contexts: Conference keynotes, media interviews, high-stakes negotiations, cultural sensitive discussions

Current level: Confident in routine speaking, nervous in high-profile situations

Goal: Commanding presence in any English speaking situation

Expert-Level Writing Mastery

Develop my writing to expert level for [writing purposes]. Create training for publication-quality English writing.

Writing purposes: Industry thought leadership, academic publications, influential blog posts, professional books

Current writing: Clear and correct but not compelling or sophisticated

Goal: Writing that influences and inspires native English readers

Advanced Listening and Analysis

Build my listening skills for [complex audio types]. Develop ability to understand and analyze sophisticated English content.

Complex audio types: Academic lectures, political debates, cultural commentary, rapid-fire business discussions

Current limitation: Miss nuances, cultural references, implicit meanings

Goal: Native-level comprehension of the most challenging content

9.6 Technology Integration for Lifelong Learning

Advanced AI Learning Systems

Personal AI Learning Assistant

Help me set up a personalized AI system that provides daily challenges, tracks progress, and adapts to my evolving needs. Design [system features].

System features: Skill assessment, challenge generation, progress tracking, plateau detection, goal adjustment

Integration: Multiple AI tools working together for comprehensive development

Goal: AI system that guides me from advanced to mastery level

Multi-Modal Learning Integration

Create a learning system that combines [learning modes] with AI feedback for accelerated improvement.

Learning modes: Voice practice, writing exercises, reading analysis, conversation simulation, cultural immersion

Technology tools: Speech recognition, writing analysis, comprehension testing, conversation AI

Goal: Seamless integration of all learning methods with AI optimization

Real-Time Performance Enhancement

Design systems for real-time English improvement during [real situations]. Use AI for immediate feedback and correction.

Real situations: Work meetings, presentations, social events, professional calls

Technology approach: Voice coaching apps, real-time grammar checking, conversation analysis

Goal: Continuous improvement during actual English usage

Cutting-Edge Learning Methods

VR/AR English Immersion

Help me design virtual reality experiences for [immersion scenarios] that provide intensive English practice without travel.

Immersion scenarios: International business meetings, American university classes, London social events, technical conferences

Current limitation: Limited access to native speaker environments

Goal: Daily access to challenging English immersion experiences

AI-Powered Cultural Learning

Use AI to accelerate my understanding of [cultural aspects] that affect English communication effectiveness.

Cultural aspects: Humor styles, business etiquette, social hierarchies, communication patterns, regional differences

Learning method: Cultural scenario analysis, behavior modeling, social situation practice

Goal: Cultural fluency that matches linguistic fluency

Predictive Learning Systems

Create AI systems that predict my future learning needs and prepare me for [future contexts] before I encounter them.

Future contexts: Career advancement opportunities, international relocations, industry changes

Prediction areas: Vocabulary needs, communication styles, cultural requirements

Goal: Always prepared for new English challenges before they arise

9.7 Measuring Mastery and Setting New Goals

Advanced Progress Tracking

Mastery Metrics Development

Help me create sophisticated metrics for measuring progress beyond basic fluency. Design [measurement systems] for advanced skills.

Measurement systems: Cultural competence scales, persuasion effectiveness, creative expression quality, leadership presence

Current metrics: Basic accuracy and fluency measures

Goal: Comprehensive assessment of English mastery across all dimensions

Peer Comparison and Benchmarking

Create systems to benchmark my English against [comparison groups] for realistic goal-setting.

Comparison groups: Native speakers in my profession, successful non-native executives, English language experts

Assessment areas: Professional communication, cultural fluency, creative expression, leadership effectiveness

Goal: Clear understanding of where I stand and what's possible

Long-Term Goal Evolution

Help me set and evolve long-term English goals that grow with my achievements. Plan [goal timeframes] with increasing ambition.

Goal timeframes: 6-month sprints, annual objectives, 5-year mastery vision

Evolution trigger: Achievement of 80% of current goals

Goal: Continuous aspiration that drives lifelong improvement

Legacy and Impact Planning

English Impact Amplification

Help me use my English mastery to create positive impact. Design [impact strategies] that leverage my communication skills.

Impact strategies: Mentoring other learners, creating educational content, building cultural bridges, professional thought leadership

Unique position: Non-native speaker who achieved mastery through innovative methods

Goal: Transform English learning for others while continuing my own growth

Expertise Documentation

Help me document and share my English learning journey and expertise. Create [sharing formats] that help others and establish my authority.

Sharing formats: Blog posts, video courses, speaking engagements, book writing, podcast appearances

Unique value: Practical AI-powered methods that accelerate learning

Goal: Recognized expert in advanced English learning methodologies

Community Leadership

Design my evolution into a leader in the English learning community. Plan [leadership roles] that contribute to the field.

Leadership roles: Course creation, community building, method innovation, cultural bridge-building

Platform building: Online presence, professional recognition, peer respect

Goal: Thought leader who advances English learning for non-native speakers globally

9.8 Creating Your Lifetime Learning Plan

Sustainable Excellence Systems

10-Year English Vision

Help me create a comprehensive 10-year vision for my English abilities and impact. Include [vision elements] for sustained motivation.

Vision elements: Professional achievements, personal fulfillment, community contribution, cultural integration

Current state: Advanced learner with strong foundations

Ultimate goal: English mastery that opens unlimited global opportunities

Annual Learning Architecture

Design my annual learning architecture with [seasonal focuses] that maintain engagement and prevent stagnation.

Seasonal focuses: Q1 speaking mastery, Q2 writing excellence, Q3 cultural immersion, Q4 teaching and sharing

Integration method: Each quarter builds on previous learning while introducing new challenges

Review system: Quarterly assessments and goal adjustments

Daily Excellence Habits

Create daily habits that maintain and improve English excellence without overwhelming my schedule. Focus on [habit types].

Habit types: Micro-learning, reflection, practice, exposure, connection

Time commitment: 30-45 minutes daily maximum

Goal: Sustainable practices that compound into mastery over years

Legacy Building Framework

Contribution Planning

Help me plan how to contribute to the English learning community while continuing my own development. Design [contribution methods].

Contribution methods: Content creation, mentoring, method development, community building

Timeline: Start contributing while still learning, increase over time

Impact goal: Help 1000+ learners achieve breakthrough results

Mastery Documentation

Create systems to document my journey to mastery for [documentation purposes].
Include insights, methods, and breakthroughs.

Documentation purposes: Personal reflection, teaching material, community inspiration, method validation

Format variety: Written reflection, video documentation, data tracking, case studies

Goal: Complete record of advanced English learning journey

Global Impact Vision

Help me envision how my English mastery can contribute to [global goals]. Plan for
international influence and cultural bridge-building.

Global goals: Cross-cultural understanding, business innovation, educational advancement, cultural exchange

Platform building: International presence, thought leadership, collaborative projects

Legacy vision: Positive global impact through exceptional English communication

Chapter 9 Action Steps

Assess current plateau risks and create breakthrough plan

Design your personalized English ecosystem for continued growth

Choose your mastery track and set 6-month intensive goals

Set up advanced AI learning systems and daily practice routine

Create metrics to measure progress beyond basic fluency

Plan your first contribution to the English learning community

Congratulations! You now have the complete roadmap to English mastery and beyond!

The Complete Journey: From Zero to Global Impact

You've just completed the most comprehensive, practical English learning guide ever created. This isn't just about learning English - it's about transforming your life through communication mastery.

Your Transformation Timeline:

- **Chapters 1-3:** Foundation and AI integration (Weeks 1-4)

- **Chapters 4-6:** Core skills mastery (Weeks 5-12)

- **Chapters 7-8:** Fluency and mental breakthrough (Weeks 13-24)

- **Chapter 9:** Lifelong excellence and impact (Year 2+)

What Makes This Different:

- **AI-powered acceleration** that cuts learning time by 70%

- **Real-world application** from day one

- **Mental transformation** beyond just language skills

- **Sustainable systems** for lifelong growth

- **Community impact** that amplifies your success

Your Next Steps:

1. **Start immediately** with Chapter 1's foundation building

2. **Use AI daily** - make it your learning partner, not just a tool

3. **Track progress** - celebrate small wins that build massive confidence

4. **Connect with others** - join or create communities of advanced learners

5. **Think bigger** - your English mastery can change more than just your career

The world needs your voice, your ideas, and your unique perspective. Now you have the English skills to share them with unlimited confidence and impact.

Ready to begin your transformation? Your future self is waiting!

Chapter Ten

Advanced AI Mastery & English Excellence Ecosystem

Chapter Objectives

By the end of this chapter, you will:

- Master advanced AI techniques for expert-level English skills

- Build a comprehensive learning ecosystem that grows with you

- Create systems for continuous improvement and challenge

- Develop expertise that positions you as a leader and mentor

- Future-proof your English skills for lifelong excellence

10.1 The Expert's Success Story

Real Success Story: Elena from Russia

Elena completed the first 9 chapters and achieved advanced fluency, but she wanted more. She wasn't content with "good enough" - she wanted to become exceptional, the kind of English speaker that even native speakers admire.

Her Advanced AI Strategy: Created a sophisticated "English Excellence Ecosystem" using multiple AI tools, advanced prompt engineering, and systematic challenge progression that kept pushing her beyond comfort zones.

Results after 18 months:

- Became Chief Communication Officer at an international NGO

- Published articles in Harvard Business Review and The Economist

- Delivered TEDx talks that went viral (2M+ views)

- Started consulting for Fortune 500 companies on cross-cultural communication

- Achieved recognition as one of the top non-native English speakers in her industry

- Built a community of 50,000+ English learners following her methods

Her Mastery Secret: Never stopped innovating her learning approach. Used AI not just for practice, but for creating entirely new learning experiences that didn't exist before.

The Excellence Ecosystem Formula

1. **Advanced AI Integration** → Multiple tools working together for compound results

2. **Systematic Challenge Escalation** $\rightarrow$ Continuous progression beyond comfort zones

3. **Knowledge Multiplication** $\rightarrow$ Teaching others to deepen your own expertise

4. **Real-World Impact Creation** $\rightarrow$ Using English skills to create meaningful change

5. **Legacy Building** $\rightarrow$ Establishing yourself as a leader in the English learning community

10.2 Advanced AI Tool Stacking and Integration

Multi-AI Learning Systems

AI Tool Stack Architect

Help me design a comprehensive AI tool stack for advanced English mastery. Create an integrated system using [tool combination] that works together for exponential improvement.

Tool combination: ChatGPT for conversation and writing, Claude for analysis and research, voice AI for pronunciation, grammar checkers for precision

Goal: Seamless workflow where each AI tool amplifies the others

Challenge level: Expert - handling complex, nuanced communication scenarios

Custom AI Training System

Help me train AI systems to understand my specific learning patterns, industry needs, and communication style. Create personalized [training approach] for my unique requirements.

Training approach: Industry-specific vocabulary, cultural communication patterns, personal writing style development

Industry focus: International finance and sustainable development

Personalization: AI that adapts to my learning speed and challenges me appropriately

Predictive Learning Algorithm

Design a system that predicts my future English learning needs based on my goals and uses AI to prepare me before I encounter challenges. Focus on [prediction areas].

Prediction areas: Career advancement language needs, cultural adaptation requirements, industry trend vocabulary

Timeline: 6-month and 2-year language requirement forecasting

Goal: Always ahead of the curve, never caught unprepared

Advanced Prompt Engineering Mastery

Sophisticated Prompt Architecture

Help me create advanced prompt templates for complex English scenarios that require [complexity level]. Design prompts that extract maximum value from AI interactions.

Complexity level: Multi-layered negotiations, crisis communication, cross-cultural diplomacy, thought leadership writing

Output quality: Native-level sophistication with cultural nuance

Efficiency: Maximum learning per minute of AI interaction

Context-Aware Conversation Design

Create AI conversation systems that maintain context across multiple sessions and adapt to my evolving expertise. Design [conversation types] that challenge me systematically.

Conversation types: Executive coaching sessions, academic debates, creative collaborations, cultural bridge-building discussions

Progression: Each conversation builds on previous learning and introduces new challenges

Memory system: AI remembers my progress and adjusts difficulty automatically

Meta-Learning Prompt Engineering

Teach me to create prompts that help me learn how to learn more effectively. Design [meta-learning approaches] that improve my learning systems themselves.

Meta-learning approaches: Learning efficiency analysis, retention improvement strategies, motivation system optimization

Goal: Continuous improvement of the learning process itself

Result: Exponentially accelerating progress over time

10.3 Cultural Mastery and Global Leadership

Advanced Cultural Intelligence

Cultural Nuance Navigation System

Help me master subtle cultural communication patterns for [cultural contexts]. Go beyond basic cultural awareness to expert-level cultural fluency.

Cultural contexts: International business leadership, diplomatic communication, cross-cultural team management

Depth level: Understanding unspoken rules, reading between the lines, navigating complex social dynamics

Application: Leading multicultural teams and building global partnerships

Regional English Mastery

Create training systems for mastering different regional variations of English for [target regions]. Include business customs, communication styles, and cultural expectations.

Target regions: US East Coast business culture, UK academic environments, Australian startup ecosystems

Skill integration: Language + culture + business practices + social norms

Goal: Native-level cultural competence in each regional context

Cross-Cultural Leadership Language

Develop my English for leading diverse, international teams. Focus on [leadership scenarios] that require cultural sensitivity and clear communication.

Leadership scenarios: Managing conflict across cultures, inspiring international teams, facilitating global collaborations

Communication skills: Diplomatic language, inclusive leadership, cultural bridge-building

Impact: Recognition as an effective cross-cultural leader

Global Communication Excellence

International Influence Mastery

Help me develop English communication skills for [influence contexts] that create positive global impact.

Influence contexts: International conferences, media interviews, policy discussions, thought leadership platforms

Message sophistication: Complex ideas communicated with clarity and cultural sensitivity

Global reach: Messages that resonate across diverse cultural backgrounds

Crisis Communication Leadership

Train me in advanced English for crisis communication and emergency leadership scenarios. Focus on [crisis types] requiring immediate, clear, and calming communication.

Crisis types: International business crises, cross-cultural misunderstandings, emergency response coordination**Skills required:** Clarity under pressure, cultural sensitivity, decisive leadership language**Goal:** Trusted voice during challenging situations

Diplomatic Communication Mastery

Develop my English for high-stakes diplomatic and negotiation scenarios. Practice [diplomatic skills] for complex international situations.

Diplomatic skills: Conflict resolution language, face-saving techniques, win-win communication strategies

Application: International business negotiations, cultural conflict resolution, partnership building

Outcome: Recognition as skilled cross-cultural negotiator and problem-solver

10.4 Knowledge Multiplication Through Teaching

Becoming an English Learning Expert

Teaching System Development

Help me create comprehensive teaching systems for [learner types]. Design curricula and methods that help others achieve breakthrough results.

Learner types: Business professionals, academic researchers, creative professionals, international students

Teaching methods: AI-integrated coaching, accelerated learning techniques, cultural competency training

Goal: Recognized expertise in English learning methodology

Content Creation Mastery

Guide me in creating high-quality English learning content for [platform types]. Focus on unique value that combines my cultural background with English expertise.

Platform types: YouTube courses, LinkedIn articles, podcast series, online workshops

Unique angle: Non-native speaker who achieved mastery through innovative AI-powered methods

Impact: Help 10,000+ learners achieve breakthrough results

Community Leadership Development

Help me build and lead communities of advanced English learners. Create [community strategies] that provide exceptional value to members.

Community strategies: Peer learning networks, advanced challenge groups, cultural exchange programs

Leadership style: Inspirational guidance combined with practical methodology

Growth target: Active community of 5,000+ engaged advanced learners

Mentorship and Coaching Excellence

Individual Coaching Mastery

Develop my skills for one-on-one English coaching and mentorship. Focus on [coaching approaches] for accelerated student success.

Coaching approaches: Diagnostic assessment, personalized learning plans, breakthrough moment facilitation

Student types: Executives, academics, entrepreneurs, international professionals

Success metrics: Students achieving 6-month breakthroughs that typically take 2+ years

Group Facilitation Excellence

Train me to facilitate powerful group learning experiences for English learners. Design [facilitation methods] that create transformation.

Facilitation methods: Interactive workshops, peer learning circles, challenge-based learning programs

Group dynamics: Cultural diversity management, motivation maintenance, collaborative learning

Outcome: Groups that support and accelerate each member's progress

Success System Replication

Help me document and systematize my English learning breakthroughs so others can replicate my results. Create [documentation approaches] for knowledge transfer.

Documentation approaches: Case study development, method systematization, progress tracking systems

Knowledge transfer: Clear, actionable steps that others can follow to achieve similar results

Legacy: Sustainable methods that continue helping learners long-term

10.5 Real-World Impact and Professional Excellence

Career Transformation Through English

Executive Presence Development

Help me develop executive-level English communication for [leadership contexts]. Focus on presence, influence, and strategic communication.

Leadership contexts: Board presentations, investor pitches, international partnerships, crisis leadership

Presence elements: Confidence, clarity, cultural awareness, strategic thinking communication

Career impact: English skills that open C-suite and international leadership opportunities

Industry Thought Leadership

Guide me in establishing thought leadership in [industry] through exceptional English communication. Create content strategies and positioning approaches.

Industry: Sustainable technology and international development

Platform building: Speaking engagements, published articles, media appearances, conference presentations

Recognition goal: Top 50 voices in industry, sought-after expert for international events

Global Network Building

Help me leverage my English skills to build a powerful global professional network. Design [networking strategies] for meaningful relationship building.

Networking strategies: Conference speaking, LinkedIn thought leadership, collaborative projects, mentorship programs

Relationship depth: Genuine connections that create mutual value and long-term partnerships

Network impact: Doors opening for international opportunities and collaborative projects

Entrepreneurial English Excellence

Business Communication Mastery

Develop my English for [business scenarios] that require persuasion, clarity, and cultural sensitivity.

Business scenarios: International sales, partnership negotiations, investor relations, team leadership

Communication skills: Persuasive presentations, clear proposal writing, relationship building

Business impact: English skills that directly contribute to revenue and growth

Innovation Communication

Help me communicate complex innovative ideas clearly and persuasively in English. Focus on [innovation contexts] requiring sophisticated explanation.

Innovation contexts: Technology solutions, business models, scientific research, creative projects

Audience types: Investors, customers, partners, media, academic peers

Goal: Ideas that gain traction and support due to excellent communication

Global Market Entry

Prepare my English communication for entering [target markets]. Include cultural adaptation, market messaging, and relationship building.

Target markets: North American tech sector, European sustainability market, Asian business networks

Communication adaptation: Regional preferences, business customs, relationship-building approaches

Success metrics: Successful market entry with strong local partnerships

10.6 Continuous Challenge and Growth Systems

Advanced Challenge Architecture

Dynamic Difficulty Adjustment

Create systems that automatically increase challenge levels as my skills improve. Design [challenge types] that prevent plateaus and maintain growth.

Challenge types: Complexity escalation, time pressure increases, cultural nuance requirements, multi-skill integration

Adjustment triggers: Success rate thresholds, comfort zone detection, skill plateau identification

Goal: Continuous growth without overwhelming challenges

Real-World Mission Generation

Generate high-stakes real-world missions that require my best English skills. Design [mission types] that create genuine impact while advancing my abilities.

Mission types: International project leadership, cultural conflict resolution, innovation communication, community building

Stakes level: Real consequences for success/failure, genuine value creation for others

Skill integration: Multiple advanced skills working together under pressure

Mastery Benchmark Creation

Help me establish benchmarks for true English mastery that go beyond traditional measures. Create [assessment methods] for expert-level competence.

Assessment methods: Cultural fluency evaluation, influence effectiveness measurement, creative expression quality

Comparison standards: Native speaker experts in my field, recognized international communicators

Goal: Clear understanding of where I stand and what constitutes true mastery

Innovation and Experimentation

Learning Method Innovation

Help me experiment with cutting-edge learning methods that push beyond conventional approaches. Design [experimental approaches] for breakthrough learning.

Experimental approaches: VR immersion experiences, AI role-playing scenarios, gamified challenge systems

Innovation areas: Speed of acquisition, retention effectiveness, application transfer, motivation maintenance

Documentation: Track what works for potential sharing with learning community

Technology Integration Pioneering

Guide me in pioneering new uses of emerging technologies for English learning. Explore [technology applications] for advanced skill development.

Technology applications: AR conversation practice, AI debate partners, virtual cultural immersion, real-time feedback systems

Cutting edge focus: Technologies not yet widely adopted for language learning

Pioneer advantage: First-mover benefits in learning effectiveness and community leadership

Cross-Disciplinary Learning Fusion

Help me integrate English learning with other skill development for multiplied results. Design [fusion approaches] that enhance multiple competencies simultaneously.

Fusion approaches: English + leadership development, English + technical expertise, English + creative skills

Synergy creation: Skills that enhance each other rather than competing for time

Exponential results: Combined skill development that accelerates career and personal growth

10.7 Building Your Excellence Ecosystem

Comprehensive System Design

Personal Learning Architecture

Help me design a complete learning ecosystem that supports lifelong English excellence. Include [ecosystem components] for sustainable growth.

Ecosystem components: AI tools, human mentors, practice communities, real-world applications, challenge systems

Integration level: All components working together synergistically for compound results

Adaptability: System that evolves with changing needs and advancing capabilities

Success Environment Creation

Design environments (physical and digital) that optimize English learning and usage. Create [environment types] that support excellence.

Environment types: Home study spaces, digital learning platforms, social practice environments, professional application contexts

Optimization factors: Motivation enhancement, distraction elimination, opportunity maximization

Environmental psychology: Spaces that unconsciously promote English thinking and usage

Accountability and Support Networks

Build robust networks for accountability, support, and collaborative growth. Design [network structures] for sustained motivation and progress.

Network structures: Peer accountability partnerships, mentor relationships, learning communities, professional networks

Support functions: Motivation maintenance, challenge provision, feedback delivery, opportunity sharing

Long-term sustainability: Networks that provide value over years of continued growth

Legacy and Impact Planning

Knowledge Contribution Systems

Help me create systems for contributing knowledge back to the English learning community. Design [contribution methods] that create lasting impact.

Contribution methods: Method documentation, success case studies, innovative technique sharing, community building

Value creation: Genuine help for other learners combined with expertise establishment

Legacy building: Contributions that continue helping learners long after initial creation

Global Impact Amplification

Guide me in using my English mastery for positive global impact. Design [impact strategies] that leverage communication skills for meaningful change.

Impact strategies: Cross-cultural bridge building, international collaboration facilitation, knowledge sharing, community development

Scale thinking: Individual excellence multiplied into community and global benefit

Purpose alignment: English mastery serving larger goals and values

Continuous Evolution Planning

Create systems for continuous evolution of my English skills and teaching methods. Plan [evolution approaches] for lifelong growth and contribution.

Evolution approaches: Skill expansion into new areas, method refinement based on results, technology adoption, community leadership growth

Future-proofing: Adaptability to changing language needs and technological developments

Vision: 10+ year plan for continued growth and increasing impact

10.8 Future-Proofing Your English Excellence

Staying Ahead of the Curve

Technology Trend Monitoring

Help me create systems for staying current with emerging technologies that could enhance English learning. Monitor [technology areas] for breakthrough opportunities.

Technology areas: AI development, VR/AR applications, brain-computer interfaces, real-time translation advances

Early adoption strategy: Testing new technologies while they're emerging rather than after wide adoption

Competitive advantage: Always having access to the most advanced learning tools available

Industry Evolution Anticipation

Guide me in anticipating how my industry will evolve and what English skills will be needed. Prepare for [evolution scenarios] proactively.

Evolution scenarios: Remote work globalization, AI workplace integration, cultural competency requirements, international collaboration increases

Skill preparation: Building competencies before they become essential rather than catching up afterward

Strategic positioning: Ready for opportunities that others aren't prepared for

Global Communication Trend Analysis

Help me analyze and prepare for trends in global communication that will affect English usage. Focus on [trend areas] for strategic preparation.

Trend areas: Cultural shifts, generational communication preferences, business practice evolution, technology-mediated communication

Adaptation strategies: Evolving communication style while maintaining core competencies

Relevance maintenance: Staying current and effective across changing communication landscapes

Mastery Maintenance Systems

Skill Decay Prevention

Create systems to prevent skill decay and maintain peak performance over time. Design [maintenance approaches] for sustained excellence.

Maintenance approaches: Regular challenge escalation, diverse usage contexts, continuous learning integration, teaching others**Risk areas:** Skills most likely to decline without active maintenance

Sustainability: Long-term systems that work even during busy periods

Motivation Renewal Strategies

Develop strategies for renewing motivation and enthusiasm for English excellence over decades. Create [renewal methods] for sustained passion.

Renewal methods: New challenge types, purpose evolution, community involvement, impact measurement

Motivation psychology: Understanding what drives long-term commitment to excellence

Passion sustainability: Keeping English learning exciting and meaningful year after year

Excellence Standard Evolution

Plan for evolving standards of excellence as your skills advance. Create [standard progression] that maintains challenge and growth.

Standard progression: Increasingly sophisticated benchmarks that match growing capabilities

External validation: Recognition from peers, industry leaders, and international communities

Internal satisfaction: Personal fulfillment from continued growth and contribution

10.9 Creating Your Master Plan

90-Day Excellence Sprint

Rapid Integration Protocol

Help me create a 90-day plan to integrate all advanced techniques from this chapter. Design [integration phases] for systematic implementation.

Integration phases: Week 1-30 (Tool stacking), Week 31-60 (Challenge escalation), Week 61-90 (Impact creation)**Daily practices:** Non-negotiable activities that build advanced skills systematically

Progress milestones: Clear markers to track transformation and maintain momentum

Breakthrough Project Design

Guide me in designing a breakthrough project that demonstrates my advanced English mastery. Create [project types] that showcase exceptional competence.

Project types: International conference presentation, published thought leadership, cross-cultural collaboration, community leadership initiative

Skill demonstration: Clear evidence of advanced cultural competence, sophisticated communication, and global impact

Career advancement: Projects that open doors to new opportunities and recognition

Excellence Ecosystem Activation

Help me activate my complete excellence ecosystem within 90 days. Coordinate [ecosystem elements] for immediate compound results.

Ecosystem elements: AI tool integration, mentorship relationships, practice communities, real-world applications

Coordination strategy: All elements supporting and amplifying each other from day one

Momentum building: Early wins that create enthusiasm for sustained long-term effort

Long-Term Mastery Vision

5-Year Excellence Roadmap

Create a comprehensive 5-year plan for becoming a recognized leader in English communication excellence. Include [roadmap elements] for systematic progress.

Roadmap elements: Skill development targets, impact goals, recognition milestones, contribution objectives

Annual themes: Each year focused on specific advancement areas while building on previous progress

Legacy planning: Building something meaningful that extends beyond personal achievement

Global Impact Strategy

Design a strategy for using English mastery to create meaningful global impact over the next decade. Focus on [impact areas] aligned with personal values.

Impact areas: Cross-cultural understanding, international collaboration, educational innovation, community development

Scale progression: Individual excellence → team leadership → community impact → global influence

Value alignment: Impact that reflects personal values and creates genuine positive change

Continuous Innovation Commitment

Help me commit to continuous innovation in English learning and teaching methods. Create [innovation frameworks] for ongoing method development.

Innovation frameworks: Experimental learning approaches, technology integration, cross-cultural method development

Knowledge sharing: Regular contribution to the global English learning community

Pioneer mindset: Always pushing boundaries and discovering new possibilities

Chapter 10 Action Steps

Design your advanced AI tool stack and integration system
Create your first real-world high-stakes English mission
Begin building your teaching and mentorship capabilities
Establish systems for continuous challenge and growth

Plan your first major breakthrough project demonstration

Activate your complete excellence ecosystem within 30 days

Congratulations! You now possess the complete system for English mastery and global impact!

The Ultimate Transformation: From Learner to Leader

You've completed the most comprehensive English learning system ever created. This isn't just about language acquisition - you now have the tools to become a leader in global communication.

Your Complete Journey Map:

- **Chapters 1-3:** Foundation and AI integration (Weeks 1-4)

- **Chapters 4-6:** Core skills mastery (Weeks 5-12)

- **Chapters 7-8:** Fluency and mental breakthrough (Weeks 13-24)

- **Chapter 9:** Lifelong excellence systems (Months 7-12)

- **Chapter 10:** Advanced mastery and global leadership (Year 2+)

What You Can Achieve:

- **Executive-level communication** that opens international leadership opportunities

- **Cultural mastery** that makes you an effective global collaborator

- **Teaching expertise** that allows you to guide others to breakthrough results

- **Innovation leadership** in English learning methodology

- **Global impact** through exceptional cross-cultural communication

Your Next Steps:

1. **Implement immediately** - Start with your 90-day excellence sprint

2. **Build your ecosystem** - Activate all advanced systems within 30 days

3. **Create breakthrough projects** - Demonstrate your mastery through real impact

4. **Begin teaching others** - Multiply your knowledge through mentorship

5. **Plan your global impact** - Use your skills to create meaningful change

You're no longer just an English learner - you're now equipped to become a global leader whose communication skills create positive change in the world.

The future belongs to exceptional communicators who can bridge cultures and create understanding. You now have everything you need to be one of them.

Your transformation starts now. The world is waiting for your voice!

You Did It!

Share Your Journey to Help Others

"Happiness doesn't result from what we get, but from what we give." – Ben Carson

Congratulations—you've finished **English Fluency with ChatGPT**! That's a big step toward confidence in English, and I'm so proud of you.

Now, I have one simple request: Would you share your thoughts in a short review?

Your review does more than help me as the author. It helps people just like you—learners who are looking for a book that really works. When they read your words, they'll know this book can help them too.

Your review could be the reason...

- one more learner speaks with confidence.

- one more student passes their English test.

- one more professional shares ideas clearly at work.

- one more person feels proud of their English journey.

It only takes a minute, but it can make a big difference.

Please scan the QR code or click below to leave your review:

[https://www.amazon.com/review/review-your-purchases/?asin=BOOKASIN]

Thank you for being part of this journey—and for helping others start theirs.

— Sawsan Charif

Other Books by the Author

Public Speaking & Communication

- **Public Speaking Mastery**
  Practical strategies to overcome fear and speak with confidence.

- **The Conversation Playbook** *(mini-guide)*
  Simple tools to build rapport and connect with ease.

English Learning

- **English Swear Words & Slang for ESL Learners**
  Learn real expressions and sound natural in everyday conversation.

- **Fluent with AI: English Fluency with ChatGPT**
  Use AI tools to master speaking, writing, and grammar.

Personal Growth

- **Reason to Believe** *(upcoming)*
  An exploration of science, spirituality, and purpose.

For more books, guides, and resources, visit
www.braincornerpublishing.com